DO ASK, DO TELL, LET'S TALK

Why and How Christians Should Have Gay Friends

Brad Hambrick
Cruciform Press | March 2016

This book is dedicated to those
who have felt that their experience of same-sex attraction
has left them isolated within or from the Body of Christ.

May this book help the church better embody
the gospel we proclaim and be the family of God.

– Brad Hambrick

CruciformPress

"This is a book the church has desperately needed for some time. It is simply excellent. It will challenge you and guide you in navigating in a more Christlike manner the host of questions surrounding same-sex attraction and the local church."

Danny Akin, President, Southeastern Baptist Theological Seminary

"To stand on what we believe is clear in Scripture, and to be a friend, at the same time – this book is an important next step for Christian literature on same-sex attraction. It doesn't simply guide us in wise engagement; it guides us in friendships where there is mutual enjoyment and appreciation. And Brad does this in such a way that he doesn't cut any theological corners but makes such friendships a necessary expression of our theology."

Ed Welch, counselor and faculty member, Christian Counseling and Educational Foundation

"Whenever Jesus encountered a sexual minority, he responded with love and friendship instead of shame. Only there, in the safety of a non-condemning presence, were these image bearers able to engage their wounds, sins and regrets. In *Do Ask, Do Tell, Let's Talk*, Brad Hambrick helps us see how we, too, can create safe space and belonging for our LGBTQ friends. And why would we do this? So that these friends, too, can encounter the grace and truth of Jesus. I highly recommend this book."

Scott Sauls, senior pastor, Christ Presbyterian Church, Nashville; author, *Jesus Outside the Lines: A Way Forward for Those Who Are Tired of Taking Sides*

"Finally, a practical book that helps us engage people as Jesus would! Brad Hambrick captures the heart of what it means to invite into dialogue and relationship people who you might otherwise see as so unlike you that you may not know how to begin a substantive conversation. Do Ask, Do Tell, Let's Talk teaches the lost art of how to talk with people, draw them out, get to know their story and, therefore, know their heart . . . all of which makes fertile soil for the gospel to take root and flourish!"

John Freeman, President, Harvest USA; author, *Hide or Seek, When Men Get Real with God about Sex*

"Let's face it, in this area the church has at best missed an opportunity and at worst grieved God through our ignorance, fear, or condemnation of not just the sin, but the person struggling. Brad Hambrick has written a much-needed response to the question, how does a Christian interact with love and help someone struggling with same-sex attraction? His book gives us an opportunity to try again, but this time we will be equipped with compassion, biblical helps, and hope. If you struggle with SSA or know someone who does, this book could start a journey toward the light of God's truth and love that will humble the helper and encourage the struggler."

Garrett Higbee, author, *The Uncommon Community: Biblical Soul Care for Small Groups*; Board Member, Biblical Counseling Coalition

"*Do Ask, Do Tell, Let's Talk* comes forth with impeccable timing to the evangelical Christian church and modern day culture by providing a pathway for engagement in safe, healing, and equipping conversations. This brief, yet comprehensive and biblically robust book gently confronts the "elephant in the room" while answering questions about friendship, homosexuality, gender identity, and same-sex attraction. I highly recommend it to men, women, students, youth workers, pastors, churches, educators, and leaders as well as anyone looking for answers to this vital topic."

Dr. Dwayne R. Bond, Lead Pastor, Wellspring Church; CEO and Founder, Proximus Group

"Few people have the ability to pack as much content into a book as my friend, Brad Hambrick. The message and content of this book is one which the church desperately needs. All of us need to be better equipped in the area of ministering and be-friending those who struggle with same-sex attraction. Brad's work is not only comprehensive and biblical, it comes from the heart of a pastor-counselor whose admirable humility in approaching a potentially polarizing topic shines through. This is the book I needed to read, and I trust it will become a go-to resource for you as well."

Jonathan Holmes, author, *The Company We Keep: In Search of Biblical Friendship*; Biblical Counseling Coalition Council Member

"If you are looking for a book that simply equips you to make a friend, love a neighbor, and if God and your friend are willing, see somebody you care about come to Christ, this is it. Winsome it is."

Sam R. Williams, Ph.D., Professor of Counseling, Southeastern Baptist Theological Seminary

Table of Contents

Introduction 7
Please Don't Skip Me

One   *Beyond the Us-Them Divide* 13

Two   *Comfortable Being Uncomfortable* 31

Three   *Learning about the Experience of SSA* . . . 47

Four   *Getting to Know a Christian*
Experiencing SSA 63
Key Markers on the Journey

Five   *Getting to Know a Non-Christian*
Experiencing SSA 81
Winning an Argument vs. Influencing
a Friend

Six   *Navigating Difficult Conversations* 101

Endnotes. 123
More books from Cruciform Press 126

CruciformPress

Books of about 100 pages
Clear, inspiring, gospel-centered
CruciformPress.com

We like to keep it simple. So we publish short, clear, useful, inexpensive books for Christians and other curious people. Books that make sense and are easy to read, even as they tackle serious subjects.

We do this because the good news of Jesus Christ—the gospel—is the only thing that actually explains why this world is so wonderful and so awful all at the same time. Even better, the gospel applies to every single area of life, and offers real answers that aren't available from any other source.

These are books you can afford, enjoy, finish easily, benefit from, and remember. Check us out and see. Then join us as part of a publishing revolution that's good news for the gospel, the church, and the world.

Do Ask, Do Tell, Let's Talk: Why and How Christians Should Have Gay Friends

Print / PDF ISBN: 978-1-941114-11-7
ePub ISBN: 978-1-941114-13-1
Mobipocket ISBN: 978-1-941114-12-4

Introduction
PLEASE DON'T SKIP ME

I love air travel.

Okay, not long TSA lines and screening. Not the part where I cram my bloated carry-on into an overhead compartment because I'm too cheap to pay the baggage fee. Not overbooked flights or weather cancellations or the mysteries of lost luggage. But the rest of it, all things considered, is pretty amazing.

My favorite part is actually the people-watching. Long layover? I got this. I'll pick up my Starbucks and a local newspaper, find a good place to sit, and enjoy the parade of humanity. Is there another public place in our society that brings together such a wide cross-section of people? In any major airport on just about any day, you'll see every imaginable ethnic, social, relational, and economic group. For introverts like me, the whole spectacle is intriguing and fascinating.

At the same time, as much as I love people-watching, I can barely imagine a scenario where I would step outside my safe personal bubble and actually go talk to a stranger. Why? Because moving toward people whom I don't know and may have little in common with makes me uncomfortable. You too?

Let's face it, not only are most of us uncomfortable around new people, we usually avoid unfamiliar situations. To one degree or another we are all creatures of comfort and familiarity. Which brings me to the subject matter of this book.

Of all the issues in the church, the one that creates the greatest amount of discomfort and diversity of opinion may be homosexuality and same-sex attraction (SSA). No doubt partly because of this, the church has yet to articulate a wise and biblical way to move toward those in our churches and communities who struggle with same-sex attraction.

Churches have articulated their position on a conservative sexual ethic. Churches have re-examined the key biblical texts that are challenged in defense of a progressive sexual ethic. As important as these things are, however, they do not equip everyday Christians to develop meaningful friendships with people who experience same-sex attraction or have embraced a gay identity.

In the absence of relationship, our theology becomes theory.

Christians are no different than anyone else in this respect: most of us don't do well with otherness. It scares us. We don't know how to relate well to people with different backgrounds and life stories. You want to have a conversation about everyday challenges like pride, being a good parent, or listening better to your spouse? We can do that. That's safe territory. But struggles with SSA? If we're brave enough to consider even having such a conversation, SSA issues can seem significantly different from our own experience. As a result, those conversations with friends and family members can become brief, awkward, and unhelpful. If they happen at all.

The sad human tendency is to see otherness—in this case, people with SSA struggles—as one-dimensional. Rather than thinking of people first as fellow image-bearers of God, we[1] essentially reduce them to their particular orientation or sexual identity. If you ask any friends and family members who struggle with SSA (and I hope you will), most will tell you their same-sex orientation encompasses something far wider than just who they are romantically interested in.

From personal observation, it seems to me that in the church we typically have one of three reactions to any sin that is markedly different from our own experience:

A. Judge/condemn it
B. Move away/isolate from it
C. Reduce/re-categorize it

Here's an example: someone in your small group brings up a wedding invitation they recently received from a gay relative. Should they attend?

A. As they're asking and seeking prayer to make a wise and biblically informed decision, one person is thinking, *Why are we even having this conversation? The Bible is clear—homosexuality is wrong! Attending this wedding would mean you support their decision to do something unbiblical.* This approach assumes that if you have the right position on sexual ethics, you automatically know how best to approach a relationship with a nephew you see twice a year or a sister you don't want to alienate.

B. Perhaps someone else in the group is having another internal dialogue along the lines of, *Phew, I'm so glad this isn't me! Sounds very complicated. I think they should just go! I want to ask more questions, because this doesn't feel so clear, but I don't want to be seen as a 'bad Christian.' Can't we just move on to another prayer request? Is it getting hot in here?* This approach assumes that not taking a position is the best way for the prospective wedding attendee to love others and facilitate that relationship.

C. For those who are inclined to reduce or re-categorize, the internal dialogue might sound like this, *Some people struggle with SSA. I experience OSA (opposite-sex attraction). I'm no better than them and they are no worse than me. We're all sinners and the good news is that Jesus died to set us both free. I don't understand what the fuss is about. Let's all repent and enjoy our lives for the glory of God.*

I suspect we have all had at least one of these reactions, and have probably struggled with what to say. The fact that you're reading this book suggests you're already aware that conversations about how to befriend and help those who experience SSA are inherently difficult for many of us.

When these kinds of conversations do happen, one side can easily get weighted towards truth-telling—*homosexuality is wrong, and is not God's design for human sexuality.* The other side of the conversation can easily get weighted toward sympathy and compassion—*it has to be hard to experience SSA, isn't there some accommodation we can make as Christians to ease their struggle?*

Unfortunately, truth apart from love is harsh and unlivable. Similarly, love apart from truth is sentimental and unhelpful. So is there another way? Can we join together truth and love in our conversations and interactions with friends who struggle and suffer differently from us? Can we honor the word of God, but also incarnate the Son of God, who was criticized for befriending the big sinners of his day (Matthew 9:11).[2] After all, big sinners—which is all of us (1 Timothy 1:15)—are exactly whom the Bible was given to.

I believe we can; I believe we should; I believe the church must. This book is an attempt to prepare God's people for rich, biblically-informed, gospel-saturated engagement that is both practical and realistic.

One
BEYOND THE US-THEM DIVIDE

Conversations on controversial issues do not to
go well when the dialogue happens community-to-
community or figurehead-to-figurehead. Whether it's
race, religion, or politics, groups don't talk well with other
groups. Too much is at stake when we feel like our words
and actions speak for the collective whole.

Two individuals from those respective groups are
much more likely to forge a good relationship, influencing one another in various ways. Unfortunately, someone
who listens well is often viewed by his or her compatriots
as engaging in compromise; at the group level, representing each side fairly feels too much like agreement.

That is why the aim of this book is friendship. Friendship is the level at which influence can be had, because
the dialogue does not seek to represent an agenda but to
understand a person. Friendship is what protects good
points from becoming gotcha moments.

I think it's important for you to know two things
about how this book is written and who is writing it.
First, this is not a book about the Christian church

reaching the gay community. Instead, it is a book about individual Christians learning to form better friendships with classmates, colleagues, and family members who experience same-sex attraction or embrace a gay identity (we will clarify those terms shortly).

How much influence will these friendships have? That will vary widely based on many factors, some of which we'll consider in the pages ahead. My encouragement to you is to seek to be a good friend (i.e., an ambassador of Christ) because influence grows best out of a flourishing friendship, not as the reason for a friendship. In fact, here's one principle that lies at the heart of this book: *Relationships always have influence, but when influence becomes the primary objective it deteriorates friendship.*

This begs the question: what is a "win" in these relationships? Is it convincing the other person to embrace a conservative sexual ethic and repent of homosexuality? Is it growing in our ability to appreciate each other's differences and refusing to judge people for things they perhaps didn't choose? (Yes, we'll talk about the matter of "choosing" homosexuality soon, as well.)

If we see these relationships as a competition—a moral or theological debate where there must be a winner and a loser—that says something. It says we believe that from the Christian perspective the only two possible outcomes in such a relationship are conversion on the other person's part or compromise on our part. That attitude will make it very hard for us to develop an authentic relationship of trust. Instead, we'll have truth wars that feel more like political debates than personal conversations.

Second, I do not consider homosexuality my hill to die on. I don't believe that the probability of experiencing the Third Great Awakening or whether America remains a geopolitical superpower hinges on the moral-political issues surrounding homosexuality. Neither do I believe that gay rights as a cause is the logical extension of women's suffrage or racial-equality efforts.

When someone holds either of these views, the rightness of their position seems so obvious that anyone taking a different view is often seen as stupid or evil. So if your position on homosexuality is approximated in the paragraph above, you may be a little uncomfortable with this book. Even if you are, I hope you'll keep reading.

With that said, in this book I have tried to recognize my "heterosexual privilege" and weigh my words accordingly. That is, because I don't experience SSA, there are many emotional and relational challenges I have simply not had to face in life. This has left me free to invest my energies in and benefit from other pursuits. Any member of a majority culture—whether the variable in question is sexual attraction, race, language barriers, economics, or something else—will tend to have a similar built-in advantage. I know this is true of me, so I hope my writing reflects that.

My experience in this subject, therefore, has primarily been as a pastoral counselor who has heard many individuals say, "I feel safe talking about SSA with you. I want to feel that way with the rest of the church." Most of these individuals have been male, so the experience I bring to this book may omit some factors that would apply more to male-female or female-female friendships. If you find yourself in one of those categories I pray you will be able to use what I have presented as a launching point and arrive at guidance that will benefit your particular friendships.

To the two challenges posed above, I would say:

1. *I believe* Christians can have and should seek meaningful friendships with those who experience same-sex attraction (SSA). The church cannot have a "don't ask, don't tell" policy and, at the same time, extend Christian love to members and neighbors who experience SSA.

2. *I recognize* the personal and theological challenges this presents. This book will not be as neat as I would like. Many tensions will be navigated; maybe not all contradictions will be avoided. When it comes to being salt and light for the sake of the gospel, it seems far better to choose possible messiness over guaranteed ineffectiveness.

3. *I acknowledge* that this is something Christians have frequently not done well with, and that even when Christians have made good attempts their efforts have not always been received well by members of the gay community. While both sides need to consider their response, I will speak to the church because that is the community to which I belong.

So let's return to the earlier question. I would consider any of the following outcomes a "win."

- An individual who embraces a gay identity could say, "I have friends who are Christians and disagree with my chosen lifestyle but love me well. I believe they would gladly help me if I had a need."

- A teenager who is beginning to experience SSA could say, "I have Christian friends who understand what I'm facing and care enough to help me think through this confusing experience."
- Parents of a child who is experimenting with homosexual behaviors could say, "Our small group cared for us well and helped us think through how to love our son. It was surprising how safe we felt to wrestle with the questions we were facing."
- An individual who was considering leaving the gay lifestyle could say, "The Christians who I knew while I was openly gay were a big part of the reason I may choose to pursue what I now believe to be God's design for sexuality."

This book will seek to equip you to help make these statements an increasing reality in the life of your church. In this chapter, we will consider two social dynamics that impede these responses:

- The role of language
- The unintended consequences of a "don't ask, don't tell" climate in the church

The Value of a Shared Vocabulary

I face a problem every time I take my car to the mechanic. I don't know what words to use. How should I describe the sound my car makes? The absence of useful language immediately makes me feel like an idiot. The confused look on my mechanic's face confirms it.

Something similar happens when we try to discuss

subjects like depression or compulsiveness. What is the difference between normal sadness and clinical depression, or between having strong pet peeves and experiencing Obsessive-Compulsive Disorder? When we're unsure what words to use—or what the words we *could* use might communicate to others—we usually become highly self-conscious…so we say nothing.

This often happens around the subject of homosexuality. Whatever words we might use can feel presumptuous, inflammatory, too condemning, too accepting, or something else. So what do we do? Usually we either avoid the subject or bulldoze through the awkwardness.

In an effort to chip away at this problem, I'm going to suggest that within the church we adopt a shared vocabulary. I believe the following three terms both correspond to reality and align with Scripture. These terms are not neutral—all distinctions have consequences. But I believe these categories give us accurate ways to think and talk about some of the key issues surrounding homosexuality, and are therefore helpful both for a) individuals confused about their sexuality[3] and b) Christians who want to have a constructive conversation on the subject.

- **Same-Sex Attraction (SSA)** – This is simply the experience of realizing that you find members of the same gender attractive to the point that you are aroused and romantically captivated. This experience is usually not chosen. Think about it: if you experience opposite-sex attraction, when did you choose this preference?

  For this reason, I believe that the best theological category for the experience of unwanted SSA is *suffering*—something for which we should not feel a perpetual sense of condemnation, because it is primarily the result of living in a broken world which adversely impacts our lives. True suffering is not sin.[4] In response to suffering, God offers comfort, not forgiveness. At the same time, suffering is always *a context for temptation*, and we are responsible for our response to suffering.

The primary benefit of the *suffering* category is that it gives the person who experiences unwanted SSA the grace to recognize that Romans 8:1 ("There is therefore now no condemnation for those who are in Christ Jesus") can be true for him or her. It allows for the possibility of stewarding temptation in a way that pleases God, rather than feeling like a perpetual abomination. Indeed, the "abomination passages" (Leviticus 18:22, 20:13) refer to homosexual *behaviors*, not people struggling against temptation. The SSA, GI, and HB distinctions help us reconcile the fact that God is indeed the holy judge of sin yet still desires to be the loving redeemer of people who struggle with sin until we reach heaven.

• **Gay Identity (GI)** – GI occurs when an individual who experiences SSA travels down a path that leads him or her to an "I am" statement. Where SSA is about "what I feel," GI is about "who I am."

This transition is where much of our cultural conversation breaks down. In any other area of life, if one aspect of personhood (such as ethnicity, financial status, gender, etc.) is believed to necessarily define a person, we call that belief prejudicial. But with sexuality, there is a cultural push to call it virtuous.

It is not necessary to turn verbs into nouns. Not everyone who runs is a runner. Not everyone who fails is a failure. Not everyone who experiences SSA has to identify as gay. Identity is a choice, one that should be made based on more factors than the persistence of a particular attraction.

- <u>**Homosexual Behavior (HB)**</u> – This is the choice to engage in sexual practices with or stimulated by a member of the same gender. Like assuming a gay identity, homosexual behavior is a matter of choice and, therefore, the moral responsibility of the chooser.

  A different kind of stigma enters the conversation here. We must realize that looking at gay porn is not "dirtier" than straight porn, and is far less consequential than looking at child porn. Extra-marital sex is equally wrong regardless of the gender-pairing. We'll consider these kinds of internal emotional obstacles in chapter two.

Categories are sterile. By themselves, they're lifeless. We must realize that we never interact with a category (e.g., homosexuality) but only a person (e.g., individuals who experience SSA). Consider the following case study.[5]

* * *

Grayson was a fun kid whose interests didn't fit in a box well. Sports were fine, but he enjoyed art and conversation more. Grayson was also an "old soul;" the banter of boys his age was not as interesting to him as the more personal conversations girls or adults were having.

When Grayson wouldn't engage the banter of his peers, they picked on him and, as elementary school progressed, he felt like more of an outsider with boys. He found interests and friendships that were satisfying, but the sense of being different marked his early school experience.

In middle school, when the other boys started talking about liking girls, this seemed odd to him. He couldn't remember disliking girls. Girls made sense to him. It was boys who were strange. A similar change occurred in him as was happening in his peers; he began to be attracted to those who he viewed as different from him. But instead of it being the opposite gender, it was the same sex.

This was unsettling. But it made exploring his interest easier. When there was a boy who was mature enough to have a meaningful conversation, he could talk with him without everyone else asking if they "liked" each other. For Grayson, it became difficult to tell the difference between friendship and romantic interest.

One thing Grayson did know is that he should not talk about this. But he did ponder it. What did this mean? Why did his body respond this way? What did this mean about who he was? How much of his life did this explain?

Grayson's family attended church regularly, so he knew that homosexuality was a sin. In sermons, homosexuals were either the bad guys in an illustration or the punch line of a joke. In high school, some of the youth leaders would talk about lust and say they were available to talk. How unfair that his sexual questions and struggles seemed off limits because they were never mentioned as a possibility?!?

When he heard friends talking about internet pornography he was curious. Soon the internet became a source of safe exploration. He discovered he did find the male body more arousing than the female body. Through blogs and on-line forums he found people who understood him. Finally there was an outlet for his questions, and people to give language to his experience.

During his first semester at college he got connected with an LGBT (lesbian, gay, bisexual, transgender) group on campus. It was the first time he had had real community (not online conversations) with real people who accepted him. He felt known, loved, and free like never before. He learned that October 11 was National Coming Out Day,[6] and he decided it was time to face whatever consequences came as he was finally honest with the world.

* * *

To help assimilate what you're learning, go back and write SSA, GI, and HB in the margin next to particular sentences in this account to help you see where the transitions took place for Grayson. Make notes of any pet theories you have used to explain why these things happen to people, or what you think should be done for Grayson at this point. Don't assume your theories are accurate or your solutions helpful. Merely allow this exercise to make your assumptions more overt, so they can be evaluated as you go through the rest of the book.

Take a moment and reflect on your reaction to reading this case study. What made you sad, angry, uncomfortable, or the like? What kinds of additions, clarifications, or qualifications did you want to see in this account?

If you feel suspicious toward or upset with Grayson

because of this brief description of his life, I submit to you that this is a sign of prejudice. Prejudice calls for repentance, so I would encourage you to seek God both for repentance and freedom from this sin. *We will never befriend those whose stories we cannot bear hearing.*

Now let's ask, "How does having a shared vocabulary (SSA, GI, and HB) allow us to foster meaningful friendship with Grayson? How does seeing his experience in its different aspects, instead of as an all-or-nothing proposition, create the opportunity for better interaction?"

For Grayson, clear language makes the church a safe place to talk. When a church is uncomfortable with how to talk about a subject redemptively, we typically ignore it. For a high-school age Grayson, for example, completely ignoring SSA would say, "You don't belong here," a message nearly as stigmatizing and ostracizing as offensive language. But the church should be a safe place for him to talk about his experience and learn how to think about it.

How can we facilitate this? In our sermons and lessons, we should include SSA in the list of things someone might be struggling with—just like lust, pride, loneliness, anger, or any other common sin. Just as importantly, our tone of voice when speaking of SSA should not communicate disgust, condescension, or perplexity.

For the church at large, clear language facilitates relatability. The categories of SSA, GI, and HB also help by allowing those who do not experience SSA to identify in certain respects with those who do. Hopefully, when you read Grayson's story, you liked him. Whether we realize it or not, we all have struggles that tend to follow a predictable progression: we go from disposition (e.g., a desire for orderliness), to identity (e.g., "I'm compulsive"), to lifestyle (e.g., living by a set of routines).

While the parallel between SSA and dispositions in general is not absolute, it can help you identify with how the experience of SSA develops into a homosexual lifestyle. See if you can fill in the chart below with any of your own experiences.

Disposition	Identity	Lifestyle
Orderliness	"I am a compulsive person."	Security rooted in following daily routines
Extroversion	"I am a people person."	Being ruled by the acceptance of others
Same-Sex Attraction	"I am gay."	Selecting a community to belong to and dating

<u>**Clear language helps us all think more clearly.**</u> A third way these categories help is that they prevent us from getting ahead of ourselves or Grayson in the conversation. In middle school, Grayson doesn't need to be deciding the trajectory for his lifelong romantic relation-

ships any more than a student needs a lecture about being homeless under a bridge the first time she experiments with alcohol.

But Grayson does need to be able to talk about the sense of attraction he feels and begin to explore how to reconcile those attractions with his faith and other core values. Christian mentors and friends should absolutely be part of this journey. You could say something like this when Grayson initially shares what he's going through:

"Grayson, you're showing a lot of courage, and I admire that. You're trusting me with something precious, and I am honored. I can understand why this feels like the biggest thing in your world right now, but I don't want you to feel like your sense of attraction has to define who you are. You've probably got more questions than I have answers: me too. I'm glad I get to be your friend and don't want you to feel alone as you consider these things."

<u>Clear language helps to keep the conversation focused on personhood.</u> A fourth way these categories help is that they allow Grayson to see that he is larger than his experience of SSA. Grayson *might* make SSA a more central part of his life by engaging in homosexual behavior and embracing a gay identity, but those are not inevitable choices.

A primary implication of this for Grayson's friends is that they should spend as much time getting to know other aspects of his life and interests as they do discussing his experience of SSA. Fixating on overcoming a struggle in any particular area can almost make that area as much a core part of your identity as if you were to stop struggling and embrace it. (Because this book focuses on understanding the experience of SSA and navigating the moral-theological challenges that surround SSA, it would be easy to see this book as contributing to this imbalance. By knowing that danger exists, however, we can help avoid it.)

What would it be like if there were a widespread habit in your church of thinking about people one-dimensionally, focusing primarily on a principal area of struggle in their lives?

- *Oh, Margaret? Isn't she that perfectionist?*
- *Maybe you've met Carlos. He's an insecure people-pleaser.*
- *Eric is a pretty good guy, for a lazy person.*

What if, in talking with others in your church, you realized that one particular area of your life dominated the conversations that people had with you or about you? At the opposite extreme, what if that area were seen as too shameful or alien even to mention?

It doesn't matter what the issue is. To effectively reduce someone to a primary area of struggle in his or her life is neither fair, accurate, nor helpful. Thus, one of the most redemptive things Christian friendships can bring to the experience of SSA is the lived experience that sexuality does not have to be either personally defining or, on the other hand, socially ignored.

Silence Leads Nowhere Good

As stigmatizing and offensive as a church's silence can be when it comes to SSA, much of evangelicalism has adopted an unspoken "don't ask, don't tell" policy. The result has been decades of silence in untold thousands of churches; silence compounded by confusion, isolation, and alienation.

It's as if we believe that having a biblical position on SSA is *the same as* providing Christian care. We don't believe this about other life struggles. We have moral positions on pornography, but we encourage accountability relationships. We have moral positions on cohabitation, but we'll offer a couple a way to live separately until they get married.

Consider this from the perspective of an individual in a local church who experiences SSA. For years this person has seen personal struggles of many kinds being addressed in the church, and care offered to those who struggle. Yet the only time his or her greatest area of struggle is mentioned is in jokes or as an example of an adversarial cultural agenda. Eventually he concludes, "This is not a safe place for me."

(Is it? Should it be? Does God want the local church be a safe place for people to be honest about their struggles?)

Then, should this person find in the gay community the voice that the church community never gave him (or her) room to express, he gets very excited and feels liberated—and we get offended by his celebratory tone. It's true: to the extent he is openly celebrating sin, that's wrong. But at one level how can we blame him for shouting? He had been silenced for years, and now he isn't. It's a bit like blaming a lame person for dancing when one day he can finally walk.

To provide a tangible example, many Christians and cultural conservatives were upset when Michael Sam, the first openly gay player to be drafted into the NFL, kissed his boyfriend on national television when he signed his contract. My son saw his kiss on Sports Center the next morning. It made him uncomfortable. I don't like it when culture forces conversations about sexuality, not just homosexuality, on kids at early ages. It eats away at their innocence at younger and younger ages, which is not good.

At the same time, I'm not surprised that Sam *wanted* to celebrate openly in that way. If we assume his SSA experience began around puberty, then by the time he came out at age 23 he had been silent for 10+ years. Yes, the kiss introduced questions of sexuality to a younger audience than would be ideal, but I don't blame Michael Sam for that any more (and much less) than I blame Hannah-Montana-turned-Miley-Cyrus for her antics.

But here's a far more important issue for us, as ambassadors of Christ. Had Michael Sam attended our church as a boy, what would we have been able to offer him when he was beginning to experience SSA? And what kind of friendships could we offer him now if he were curious about exploring Christianity?

The answer cannot begin with, "Let's get him into counseling or a recovery group." Either may be beneficial, as they are for any identity-based struggle. But if this is the church's answer, it communicates, "Stick with *your people* and we'll relate to you when you're *better.*"

The best and most helpful thing the church could and must provide is *friendship*. Yes, church membership may be a delicate subject if someone is engaging HB or embracing a GI, but welcomed church participation should not be. The church, if it is to represent Christ accurately, must offer a quality of friendship that allows those who experience SSA to be more fully known and more fully loved in the church than they could find in the gay community. We should want to offer our gay friends such meaningful friendship that the memory of it can be used by God to draw them to himself (Romans 2:4).

I realize the church is not there yet. In fact, many Christians are seeing that the church's unwillingness to befriend people who experience SSA has blocked us from engaging with the subject of homosexuality on any level closer than the political. Indeed, in some respects the church as a whole is quite bad at real, biblical friendship.

That said, this book is not about friendship *per se* — it is an examination of the unique challenges SSA can present to friendship in Christian circles. For a solid understanding of what constitutes real friendship and how to get there, let me recommend Jonathan Holmes' book, *The Company We Keep: In Search of Biblical Friendship*. The fact is that friendship is a more meaningful, less casual relationship than is commonly thought, and most of us are far less equipped to be good friends than we probably have assumed. Jonathan's book is an excellent introduction to what God meant friendship to be. In fact, I hope that the more you read this book, the more compelled you'll be to read that one.

Ultimately, though, I hope this book will be a tool God uses to grow his people into excellent ambassador-friends to their classmates, colleagues, and family members who experience SSA. I trust that if this is what you want to do and be, then God will be faithful to complete this work in you regardless of the strengths and weaknesses, insights and oversights of this book (Philippians 1:6). Thank you for taking this journey with me.

Two
COMFORTABLE BEING UNCOMFORTABLE

As a kid who got picked on in high school for enjoying math, I'm fascinated by the story of Alan Turing. Turing was a mathematical genius who led the Allied efforts to decode encrypted messages from the German Nazis during World War II. It is estimated that his efforts shortened the war by two to four years and saved countless lives. His pioneering work was foundational for both computer science and artificial intelligence. Without question, Turing played a huge role in changing the course of human history.

What happened next, however, grieves me deeply. After the war, the public learned that Turing was a practicing homosexual. Because homosexual acts were illegal in the United Kingdom, his social status immediately flipped from national hero to despised criminal. He was convicted of sexual crimes and stripped of his security clearances and the honors he had earned for his invaluable contributions to ending WWII. For his sentence, Turing chose chemical castration over prison. Two years later he committed suicide. In 2013, Queen Elizabeth II apologized on behalf of the British government for "the appalling way he was treated" and granted him a posthumous pardon.

What should we take from these tragic events? At the very least, we should grieve the senseless death and public shaming of someone who used his gifts to serve the world so well. We could emphasize that not everything immoral should be illegal. But most beneficial, at least in my estimation, we could allow Turing's story to reveal the need of Christians to acknowledge our internal biases related to homosexuality.[7] And we could do this to help equip ourselves to become better, more Christ-like friends.

For better or worse, many people are uncomfortable talking about sexuality. (The better motivations involve modesty and innocence; the worse, ignorance or prejudice.) For some, our first experience of people talking openly about sex was a middle-school locker room. Indeed, people who are comfortable talking about sex are generally considered crude or immature. (This is why "the talk" our parents had with some of us about sex likely offered far less than we needed to know.) Whatever the cause of our discomfort in this area, it places us at a disadvantage when it comes to befriending those who experience SSA.

> **Reflect:** Do any tasteless or offensive jokes or anecdotes come to mind when you consider homosexuality? Are you willing to write them down?[8] This is not meant to produce shame but repentance. The point is to help us acknowledge where and how we need to mature.

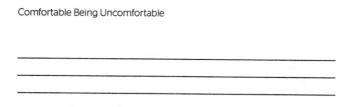

For some readers it may feel as though we're beginning to disobey Ephesians 5:12, "For it is shameful even to speak of the things that they do in secret" (referring generically to anyone who commits "unfruitful works of darkness" v 11). But it is clear that Paul was not forbidding Christians from speaking about homosexuality itself. That would mean some sins are off-limits for direct Christian care. Indeed, Paul even wrote public letters addressing the subject.

What we should avoid is talking about or describing sinful homosexual acts in the wrong *way* or with wrong *motivation*. The wrong *way* aggrandizes the sin, drawing undue attention and lending a kind of false glory to what Paul reminds us is "shameful." The wrong *motivation* draws attention to ourselves, generally by a desire to build social capital off our "frankness," or even worse, through tasteless and offensive jokes.

Either way, drawing attention to sin for non-redemptive purposes is wrong. We can honor Ephesians 5:12 without being silent, harsh, permissive, or distant on the subject of SSA.

Granted, this is not always easy. When someone begins to identify themselves by their sexuality, it is hard not to think about the sexual aspects. This is not meant to be a crude comment. It merely acknowledges a reality that does not come into play when we're talking to someone of another career, ethnicity, or religion. But most of us have had to get over this awkwardness about sexuality before. It is a more-pronounced version of the discomfort we likely felt when we realized our parents were having sex and we knew what that meant.

Again, the same-sex aspect admittedly increases this awkwardness, especially when combined with ignorance about SSA. I am reminded of the teenage boy who said to me, "Now that I've told my parents I'm attracted to other guys, they're freaking out like I'm a sex addict. They're treating me like I'm a slut with no values and I want to sleep with every guy I see."

Unfortunately, this wasn't an isolated instance of poorly informed parents. It represents a false theology of homosexuality that is common in the church, despite being based on unspoken misconceptions rather than biblical teaching. My goal in this chapter is to:

1. Put this false theology into words,
2. So that it can be critiqued, and then
3. Examine its unintended consequences.

I hope this will help you see where this false theology may have created internal obstacles to the development of friendships with those who experience SSA. Moreover, I hope it will help you navigate those obstacles with greater maturity once you're able to articulate them.

The Romans One Road

Within the evangelical church there is a common (although not universal), yet misguided interpretation of Romans 1:24-27. It is, from my perspective, an overly broad interpretation that unfortunately undergirds much of the internal resistance that Christians experience when it comes to the idea of having gay friends. You may not see Romans 1:24-27 this way, but many well-intentioned Christians do. Let's revisit the passage.

> Therefore God gave them up in the lusts of their hearts to impurity, to the dishonoring of their bodies among themselves, because they exchanged the truth about God for a lie and worshiped and served the creature rather than the Creator, who is blessed forever! Amen.
> For this reason God gave them up to dishonorable passions. For their women exchanged natural relations for those that are contrary to nature; and the men likewise gave up natural relations with women and were consumed with passion for one another, men committing shameless acts with men and receiving in themselves the due penalty for their error. (Romans 1:24-27)

In the interpretation I'm referring to, this passage supposedly teaches that SSA *only* happens when someone persistently pursues heterosexual sex outside of marriage. In some of these cases, God then judges that person by allowing his or her sexual interests to become homosexual in nature. In brief form, the logic of this "progressive sexual depravity" model goes something like this.

1. All sexual sin starts out as heterosexual. It is assumed the general effects of the Fall *cannot* distort our drive for "natural relations" into those "contrary to nature" without our escalating, willful participation in heterosexual sin over a period of time.

2. Milder heterosexual sin increases in intensity, frequency, and duration in order to have the same satisfying effect.
3. With time, ever more egregious sexual sins are needed to get the same "high." The assumption here is that the goal is the rush of orgasm rather than the comfort of intimacy.
4. Eventually, homosexual sins are experimented with as a new, more stimulating experience.
5. What began as homosexual or bisexual experimentation becomes an orientation as God gives them over to their lusts. The belief is that apart from this pattern—this addiction model—there can be no such thing as SSA.

If you accept this interpretation, you will be strongly inclined to see *all* instances of SSA as proof of God's judgment. You will then likely find yourself siding "with God" and "against the gays." In fact, there are three key components of this theology that, not surprisingly, undermine the willingness and ability of Christians to form friendships with those who experience SSA:

- SSA is viewed as a form of out-of-control sexual addiction; more like heroin and cocaine than alcohol or cigarettes.
- The individual who experiences SSA is seen as being on the brink of sins such as bestiality or pedophilia.
- Therefore, those who experience SSA are responded to as "unsafe" for casual relationships.

Reflect: How much has a "progressive sexual depravity" mindset impacted your response to homosexuality?

_____

_____

_____

_____

This raises three important questions.

Am I saying that no one takes the Romans 1 road to homosexuality? No. Some people do take that road, but they are a minority. Most people who experience SSA do not take the kind of steps outlined above.

Am I saying that the Bible is wrong or "off" on this point? No. Particularly in a Roman context, where worship practices for the various gods involved many immoral sexual rituals, this path to SSA would have been relatively common. In our day, it is not temple worship in adulthood but internet pornography in adolescence that would typically contribute to this path.

It is wise to remember that the Bible's clearest passage on a subject is not always its most pertinent. If that were the case, then the main thing the Bible would say to women is to submit and wear a hat, and the main thing the Bible would say about greeting guests at church is "pucker up."

Am I saying that the Bible's teachings that homosexuality is a sin and that sex was designed to be a cross-gender, in-marriage experience are wrong? My answer to that question is No.

If the Romans 1 Road perspective I've described represents an error, then SSA *can* emerge as part of the Fall, and initially is a matter of suffering which, as we discussed in chapter one, becomes a context for temptation to sin. Because I believe SSA can emerge in this way, I also believe we can (and should) learn from those who experience SSA. Christians who experience OSA can learn how to think about the challenges of our SSA friends and then better apply Scripture based upon what we've learned. That is a primary reason I have written this book.

Am I saying that friendship is all that is needed? What about counseling? That's for your friend to decide. Whatever additional help your friend may choose to pursue will only be as effective as the quality of his or her authentic relationships outside of counseling. Counseling without friendship is like being stranded in the ocean and given a raft for one hour a week but asked to swim the other 167 hours.

Other Internal Obstacles

Unwritten theology is not our only internal obstacle. There are other social and emotional obstacles that make us uncomfortable. Let's look at five other obstacles, examining how each presents an opportunity for us to grow in our personal maturity and ministry effectiveness.

"I don't like having conversations about problems I can't fix."

Many people think that struggles are primarily shared so that they can be fixed. If they can't "fix it," they feel like they've been a bad friend. But it is good for us to have conversations when we don't know what to say. This is part of the essence of being a growing person. When we're not having conversations that challenge us to think about new things, we will commit sins either of pride or apathy.

We should always be praying that God will bring people into our lives who will provide the opportunity for us to ask new and important questions. If after reading and applying this book, you find yourself in a situation where you need to learn more, consider the following resources:

- *Homosexuality and the Christian: A Guide for Parents, Pastors, and Friends* by Mark Yarhouse
- *The Secret Thoughts of an Unlikely Convert* by Rosaria Butterfield
- *Is God anti-gay?* by Sam Allberry
- *What Does the Bible Really Teach about Homosexuality?* by Kevin DeYoung

But don't think you'll find the "answer" to "fix" SSA in any of these books. These authors were selected in part because of their humility in not making such a claim.

Think of it this way: your willingness to enter a conversation for which you do not have an answer is the only way to authentically engage the experience of the person you are befriending. You don't end a journey with an answer; their struggle is not a riddle to solve but a life to live. Walk with them!

"People may think I'm gay."

Let's be honest. We don't want to ask someone if he or she experiences SSA for the same reason they don't want to volunteer it: we both fear the awkwardness, stigma, misunderstanding, and rejection that could follow. We fear that any kind of association with even the subject of SSA could reflect badly on us and harm our reputation. In that respect, we're far more like our friend who experiences SSA than we might have thought.

In light of this point of internal resistance, take a moment and read Matthew 9:10-13.

> And as Jesus reclined at table in the house, behold, many tax collectors and sinners came and were reclining with Jesus and his disciples. And when the Pharisees saw this, they said to his disciples, "Why does your teacher eat with tax collectors and sinners?" But when he heard it, he said, "Those who are well have no need of a physician, but those who are sick. Go and learn what this means, 'I desire mercy, and not sacrifice.' For I came not to call the righteous, but sinners."

Jesus was willing to sacrifice his reputation for the sake of those he wanted to hear the gospel. Not to sound too stereotypically therapeutic, but when we allow concern for our reputation to block us from reaching out, it's probably just our "inner Pharisee" talking. And let's not forget that, objectively speaking, the social risk we take in seeking to befriend someone who experiences SSA is far smaller than the social risk he or she would take by entrusting us with that secret.

* * *

I recognize that using this passage in reference to those who have embraced a gay identity will likely be offensive.

Hopefully, by this point in this book, you can tell I am not trying to reinforce the "sizing of sin" but am speaking to those for whom this kind of thinking is an obstacle.

Even if you experience SSA and you're not open to embracing God's design for sexuality, I hope you'll continue reading. More than that, I hope you'll continue to have conversations with Christians who can embody the heart of this book for you. Books are more impersonal than friendship; I recognize and regret the necessary limitations of this medium.

✻ ✻ ✻

"If I don't know the answer, do I have to change my views?"

We must counter the *gotcha* mentality, where every conversation is a battle over debate points. It is doubtful either of you will substantively change your views on sexual ethics because you got stumped in a single conversation. If these interactions feel like debates, you're not developing a friendship.

You can tell the *gotcha* mentality has taken hold when there is a competition over framing the discussion, or over whose questions get answered first (more on this in chapter five). There may be some limited value to these kinds of conversations, but I want to be clear that debate-style interactions will not be addressed in this book; it's about friendship not keeping score.

Your friend will ask really good questions. Chances are, if SSA is not your experience, you will feel stumped by some of those questions; some will intellectually stump you (not sure how to answer), others will emotionally stump you (wishing, for their sake, there was an easier biblical way). The better you listen, the more this will be true.

Experience all of this with your friend. Seeing a child slowly die of cancer challenges our faith. Watching a pastor leave his family for another woman challenges our faith. The repetitiveness and mundane nature of everyday life challenges our faith. Why do we think SSA would be any different?

It is not ease that strengthens our faith. It is prayerfully studying Scripture while fulfilling God's mission that grows our faith. Allow the resources listed above to guide you on this journey as you humbly walk with your friend. Recognize that neither of you will be fully satisfied with the conclusions available in a broken world. Instead, when reason has done all it can, both of you will place your faith in some final arbiter for the tensions that remain.

"I might be offensive and not know it."

This is the honest fear of ignorance. It is the fear of missionaries when they enter a foreign culture. It is the fear of children who are moving to a new school. It is the fear that exists when racial reconciliation moves from theory to your living room.

The reality is you may be offensive without knowing it, but that doesn't make passivity wise. What if, instead of avoidance, we led with admission: "You know, I haven't had many friends who experience SSA. I feel like this is an area where my inexperience could easily lead me to frame questions poorly or make assumptions based on stereotypes. Can I apologize in advance and ask that if I do those things that you let me know and trust my intentions were good? I will do my best not to be defensive, but to listen well when you bring something like that to my attention."

Does this concede significant ground in the conversations that will ensue? Yes. In a debate this would be a horrible strategy. If you were trying to convince an audience, it would be like arguing with one arm tied behind your back. But this book is not about a community-versus-community encounter. It's about friendship, and in friendship, influence requires mutual trust.

"Doesn't the Bible say not to associate with sinners?"

There are many kind-hearted, Bible-believing Christians who feel that passages like 1 Corinthians 5:9-13 compel them not to befriend those who experience SSA; their motive is not hate toward another person but faithfulness toward God.

> I wrote to you in my letter not to associate with sexually immoral people—not at all meaning the sexually immoral of this world, or the greedy and swindlers, or idolaters, since then you would need to go out of the world. But now I am writing to you not to associate with anyone who bears the name of brother if he is guilty of sexual immorality or greed, or is an idolater, reviler, drunkard, or swindler—not even to eat with such a one. For what have I to do with judging outsiders? Is it not those inside the church whom you are to judge? God judges those outside. "Purge the evil person from among you." (1 Corinthians 5:9-13)

First, let's note that greed, idolatry, foul speech, and shady business deals are on this same list. Second, let's define when this passage is relevant. The chart below represents the various options available for when to apply the action steps of this passage.

	Non-Christian	Exploring Faith	Professing Christian
Experiencing temptation			
Succumbing to temptation			
Repeatedly falling to temptation			I Cor. 5:9-13
No longer calling the tempting action wrong			I Cor. 5:9-13

The white boxes represent situations where friendship is not only permissible but is encouraged by Scripture. The less frequently and more poorly we engage in friendship in the white spaces, the more that Christians who experience SSA will only become known late in their experience with SSA and receive Christian care (friendship or pastoral guidance) after their beliefs and life practices are addressed by 1 Corinthian 5:9-13. If any member of our church gets to this point in their journey with any life struggle and we, as a church, have not given them an outlet to be known and receive care, we have let them down.

The black box represents the clearest situation in which 1 Corinthians 5:9-13 is applicable. If a professing

Christian is closed to the teaching of Scripture, then there comes a point at which 1) continued fellowship constitutes a poor stewardship of a church member's time and 2) the contention produced by further dialogue/debate can only diminish the reputation of the church.

The gray box represents a church-discipline context. If someone is living in repeated sin, then the relationship becomes more focused on calls for change than on casual fellowship. This is not cutting off relationship, but it does represent a different tone of interaction than everyday friendship.

By this point in the book, I hope you are beginning to see how much of the experience of SSA fits in the white spaces. Indeed, this book is about the white spaces. Later we will explore many questions surrounding difficult relationship scenarios. But first, in the next few chapters, I want to help you build your "white space skills" by offering additional guidance on how to get to know your friend and thereby exercise influence through conversation and friendship not debate.

Three
LEARNING ABOUT THE EXPERIENCE OF SSA

It's not much of an exaggeration to say that the whole world runs on shared experience—every nation, economy, society, tribe, family, company, church, team, club, and friendship. We more easily like people who are like us, have a similar worldview, and lead similar lives. Shared experience draws us together. It's unifying. It's comfortingly familiar. But an absence of shared experience can create a sense of distance, mistrust, or even alienation.

So if you would like to understand a person whose experience is different from yours, you have to be prepared to do some work. If your experience and mine don't quite line up, our assumptions and fears can quickly gain too much influence. We can probably close smaller gaps with a little healthy conversation. But when the gaps seem large, the patient sacrifice of listening and understanding gets more difficult. That's when we typically "love from afar" (in the abstract, without really knowing the person)—delegating the task of love and kindness to others.

Here's a small example. Recently I was talking with a friend about writing this book. When I said I wanted to help remove barriers that keep Christians from building friendships with those who experience SSA, his response was, "Why?" I tried to explain further, but he simply shook his head and said, "I just don't get it. It doesn't make sense to me."

I could have left the conversation there, but I wanted to understand his perspective better, especially since nearly everyone else I've talked with about this book has responded positively. After affirming his honesty, I tried explaining again the idea behind the book, but he concluded rather firmly, "Well, that's not for me."

I eventually realized that he saw the idea of "understanding the SSA experience and befriending a person" as synonymous with "accepting the gay lifestyle as legitimate before God." He couldn't see how the "niceness" I advocated was different from theological liberalism. In his case, he couldn't see it because he had never witnessed it, so he had trouble imagining such a friendship that didn't constitute compromise.

If Christians who experience OSA want to befriend those who struggle with SSA, we have to be willing to try to understand their experience. There is a sense in which the message of the biblical gospel poses greater challenges for those who experience SSA than for others (we will discuss this later in the book). Whether you are talking with a non-believer considering embracing the gospel for the first time or a believer seeking to apply the gospel to their unwanted SSA, you can't expect this individual, during a personal conversation with you, to be receptive to a life-altering message if you have made no real effort to understand him or her. That's hardly a personal conversation at all; it's more like a lecture. Think about it: who is going to seriously consider a life-changing message from someone who intentionally resists knowing what their life is like?

That said, you will likely be surprised at how much you have in common with those who experience SSA. Yes, SSA and OSA *are* different experiences, but overall the commonality of human experience means we're more alike than we are different.

So, how do we start understanding what the SSA struggle is like? In this chapter we will consider three aspects of the experience of SSA.

- The Experience of Secrets
- The Experience of "I Didn't Choose This"
- The Experience of "It's not Primarily about Sex"

The Experience of Secrets

Secrets. Their very nature means we rarely talk about them, yet we all have them. Some are ordinary and mundane: you forgot to brush your teeth this morning, so instead you pop in a piece of gum. Others will intentionally come to light soon enough: Sue's surprise birthday party.

There's another kind of secret, though: a secret hidden because of shame. The kind of secret where, if you shared it, your life would change. A friend of mine tells this delightful story from his sophomore year of high school.

* * *

It began in Mrs. Stover's English class when she assigned a simple three-page book review of Charles Dickens' Great Expectations.

It seemed everyone was procrastinating on putting together their book reports, and about a week before the deadline one of my friends quipped, "If you liked it so much, why don't you write mine for me!" That little statement was the beginning of the end. When asked how much he would be willing to pay he replied, "$20."

By the end of the day word had spread that I was willing to write the book report for a measly $20! Orders started piling up. I don't remember exactly how many I ended up writing, but suffice it to say I had a nice wad of cash and a new appreciation for Dickens' finest work.

A few days after the reports were turned in, the principal called me into his office alongside two other boys in my class. Immediately my heart fell to the floor like a ton of bricks. I knew the secret I was hiding, and I knew the penalty if said secret were to come to light: a three-day suspension.

However, more than that, I knew if my secret was to come to light, it would mean the loss of my reputation, my standing, my identity; you see I was a very good kid in school.

After we all sat down, the principal produced three copies of our book reports. After reading through some similar portions in our reports, he stared, for what seemed like an eternity, at me and my friends. The next thing that happened is unexplainable. I'll take it as the mercy of God on my young life. The bell rang, and my principal, who taught a class, got up and said he would finish this conversation after class.

But that conversation never came! Either he forgot or he chose not to bring us back in. It seems in retrospect like such a silly situation, but for a high-school teenager whose grades and reputation meant everything, I was petrified that I would be discovered as a cheater.

* * *

A fundamental starting point to understanding the experience of many with SSA is this: *They have carried a secret which, if others knew, could completely alter their lives. A secret of such power and magnitude that it has likely controlled and colored every relationship.*

Consider my friend. Did his secret about the Dickens reports decrease his parent's love for him? No, his parents weren't even aware. Did it decrease his capacity to receive their love? Yes. Every "I love you" from his parents had to face the inner question, *Would you love me if you knew I cheated?* Every "You're such a good student" from a teacher was met with the thought, *No, I'm not. I'm a fraud.*

This is the power of a secret. Secrets can create doubts that eat away like acid at our ability to enjoy any good thing. Every compliment has an internal rebuttal. Every blessing feels undeserved. Moments of peace feel like episodes of denial or wishful thinking.

Secrets can haunt us, too. Imagine my friend's parents saying, "I need to ask you about something." What would likely be his first thought? *Did they find out?!?* Secrets seep into every neutral experience, second-guessing, accusing, and haunting us, sometimes forever.

An Exercise in Relating

First. Think of a secret you've long held on to. At the risk of making you uncomfortable, can I ask you write it down?

_____

_____

_____

_____

Second. Now imagine what it would be like for that secret to come to light. Many of us, in certain respects, *want* to be found out. At some level, perhaps ambivalently, we desire discovery and exposure. Carrying a secret is exhausting and we want to be relieved of our burden. At the beginning the exposure is excruciating, yet relieving.

In fact, consider what it would take for you to willingly disclose your deepest secret. Write out the thoughts and emotions you would experience at the thought of talking about it openly to your pastor, small-group leader, parents, spouse, or best friend.

_____

_____

_____

_____

Third. Now, multiply that feeling by the social stigma of SSA, and you've begun to approach the challenge of what you're inviting a friend to do. Would you find that kind of exposure difficult? Among other things, this book is about making it easier.

When You are the First to Know

Many who struggle with SSA have carried their secret since puberty, and possibly earlier. Being known is an incredibly scary step but a necessary one toward relief. One friend confessed to me that he had been carrying his secret burden of struggling with SSA for more than 25 years. After telling just one person, he said it was as if a weight had been lifted off him and that he was finally able to think clearly—his secret was no longer filtering and haunting every interaction. He said that harboring his secret had been like living in prison. (The "coming out of the closet" metaphor emerges from a painful, difficult reality.)

Some in the church may think this initial confession and disclosure doesn't have to be such a big deal: *If it's necessary, why focus on it being intimidating?* But we must begin with an awareness of just how hard this is for most people who struggle with SSA. If we want to have any real hope of building Christ-centered friendships with someone who experiences SSA, we need to appreciate the weight of these moments of disclosure and vulnerability.

- We must be ready to respond, not with disgust, but with dialogue.
- We must be ready to listen not to lecture.
- We must be ready to be compassionate not condescending.
- We must be ready to cry and weep rather than condemn and warn.[9]

If you are the first person that someone who experiences SSA opens up to, you have been given an amazing gift and bear a special stewardship. The wisest and most appropriate response would be, "Thank you for trusting and sharing with me." Indeed, your response in these first few moments will be critical:

- If you pull away, you will communicate to them that they've just made a horrible mistake by confiding in you.
- If you condemn or lecture them, your self-righteousness will likely push them away from you, the church, and Christ.
- If you brush over their concerns or offer up platitudes and sentimental one-liners, you're likely to communicate that the church doesn't have anything valuable to offer them, after all.
- *However*, if you take that critical moment to begin to engage them in a meaningful relationship grounded in the infinitely rich truths of the gospel, you're likely to have a friend for life.

The Experience of "I Did Not Choose This"

When to some degree we can relate to another person's experiences, it helps us wisely move toward them in love. When we realize the courage required to move from secrecy to vulnerability, it helps us appreciate those initial moments of disclosure. But there is a another realization we must bring to these conversations and relationships: almost no one actually chooses same-sex attraction. Indeed, based on my counseling experience, study, and conversations with other pastors and counselors, I'm convinced that most—probably the vast majority—of those who struggle with SSA did not choose this preference.

In many conservative churches the standard view regarding homosexuality has historically been that it is a *choice*—a sinful one. When that's your starting point, you will believe that repenting of that sinful choice is a central and essential element in the process of change. Indeed, you will see the solution as possibly difficult but nevertheless fairly straightforward, even simple in some respects. The person experiencing SSA must study Scripture, pray, and repent before God so that he or she might *stop* being attracted to people of the same sex and *start* being attracted to people of the opposite sex.

The logic makes a certain amount of sense, especially if someone who experiences SSA is appealing to the church to help them stop. But let's be honest about how difficult it is to set aside those things we know are displeasing to God. Is it easy to stop smoking, or to stop eating the wrong foods, or to consistently exercise patience toward our kids? Is it easy to consistently love your neighbor as yourself, or to stop being proud, or anxious, or angry, or lustful, or self-righteous, or any of the other sins that so easily beset us? How often do we once and for all repent of these things that we sincerely want to be free of, and they simply go away? Occasionally, but not often.

In a great many churches, any talk about being "born with" same-sex attraction is seen as caving in to the liberal left's agenda to distract us from the biblical idea of personal responsibility.[10] This message says to those who struggle with SSA: *you had a choice, you made the wrong choice, so now you can make the right choice. That should fix it.*

In other conservative churches, the subject of homosexuality is never even mentioned. Here the message is equally clear. *Surely no one at our church could possibly struggle with this. Our people aren't like that.* Of course this is equally ineffective, not to mention offensive and willfully naïve.

So let me be clear:

- Based on my friendships with those who experience SSA, one of the things they most want their Christian friends to know is that they did not choose this struggle; it is an unwanted struggle.
- I have never met anyone who said they willingly chose the path of SSA.
- I have yet to meet anyone who experiences SSA and would not prefer to be heterosexually attracted.

I know my personal experience is biased by my church setting, but in the conversations I've had, my friends who experience SSA would prefer to have an opposite-sex spouse, raise biological children, and avoid social stigma.

As I see it, the problem in the evangelical church in this area is fairly clear. Our conversations on this topic are primarily political and ethical in nature. They exist in the abstract. Therefore, if we even consider the struggles of actual people, we tend to apply simplistic, abstract solutions that we wouldn't offer for other struggles. Why? First, because quick-fix solutions don't work. But second, and more to the point, because those more everyday struggles are not laden with social and political baggage. They are not wrapped up in the culture wars, so it's far easier to apply the gospel of grace without fear of theological compromise.

In a church climate where the conversation surrounding SSA is political and ethical in nature, the person
who struggles with SSA senses that his or her admission
will essentially be used as leverage: "If you don't want to
be this way, and you want an opposite-gendered spouse,
then do something about it."

But we can't make someone change. We can't reason
someone to a different sense of attraction. It is impossible
to usurp the will of another without becoming sinfully
controlling or offensive. Yet with SSA, the will is not
typically the problem. At least in the conversations I've
had, the will is on the side of opposite sex attraction; it's
the affections that won't play along.

Besides, leverage doesn't help people change.
Influence—love empowered by trust—does.[11] Leverage is
about external behavioral change in a context of mistrust.
But influence is about internal heart change in a context of
trust. Whatever role God wants us to play in our friend's
life will be had through influence not leverage.

You might believe that discovering the origin or cause
of someone's SSA is a critical component to building a
relationship. But focusing on this area tends to make your
friendship more therapeutic than relational. My goal
in this book is to help you be a *friend*, not a counselor.
When you're talking to someone who experiences SSA,
factors like an absent or abusive father, a history of sexual
abuse, or non-gender-stereotypical interests (to list a few
popular but often misleading theories) may or may not
be contributing to their struggle. In any event, your role
is not to "solve" or "counter" those influences. Your role
is to be a safe place, one where the experience of SSA is
not the most important thing about them. Your role is to

demonstrate that they have a friend who will pursue God with them and be an oasis from the pressure to discover or resolve the nagging questions about where this undesired inclination came from.

Think about it. Does knowing the biology of puberty make it easier to be a teenager? Does knowing the choices that led to bankruptcy make budgeting easier? Does knowing your family history of addiction or impatience make self-control easier? For some people, maybe a little. But...does having a faithful friend who is clearly for you in your struggle make it easier? Yes! Now imagine that this friend comes to know the origin of your struggle naturally (to the degree it can be discerned), through conversation instead of through investigation. Imagine that he or she is willing to be your friend in ways that have nothing to do with your struggle, while providing encouragement and accountability *for* your struggle. How much better is that than a relative stranger taking you through question after troubling question?

When we realize that *so many of our experiences and inclinations are not mere choice*, but are also powerfully and inevitably influenced by biology (our fallen bodies), culture (our fallen world), and sociology (fallen people), we can begin to engage others with greater patience and compassion. And this better equips us to offer wise encouragement that can actually be received.

For the person who experiences SSA, we must keep a tangle of factors in mind, factors that are not as neat as we would like, but accurately represent the messiness of living as broken people in a broken world. When SSA is embraced by assuming a gay identity or enacted through homosexual behavior it becomes willful sin that calls for post-sin repentance. However, unwanted SSA, as a form of temptation or suffering, manifests how the fall affects our bodies and souls and calls us to continual pre-sin reliance on God for the strength, clarity, and encouragement that we all need daily. Both sin and suffering call for our empathy, love, and friendship in ways that best represent God, based on where we or our friend are in relation to our struggles.

The Experience of "It's Not Primarily about Sex"

What else do we need to know about the experience of SSA?

As we've seen, we need to understand the weight and impact of secrets. We need to know that conversations which focus on the origin of one's SSA are typically unfruitful because they tend to mutate friendship into therapy. Finally, we need to understand that SSA is not primarily about sex.

Rosaria Butterfield, who formerly identified herself as a lesbian, explains, "Sexuality isn't about what we do in bed. Sexuality encompasses a whole range of needs, demands, and desires. Sexuality is more a symptom of our life's condition than a cause, more a consequence than an origin."[12]

Indeed, I have often heard SSA strugglers emphasize, "It's not really about who I want to have sex with." Sexual attraction certainly plays a role in SSA, but it's not typically a primary focus. It's also about emotional connection, whom you feel most comfortable around, and whose companionship is more satisfying. It's about relatability and security. Just as eating disorders are about far more than food, so is SSA about far more than sex.

Many men who struggle with SSA talk about feeling alienated or isolated from male peers. In a counter-intuitive way, this alienation can lead to an increased desire for male approval and relationship. One person who experiences SSA explains, "as I entered adolescence, I became aware of an increasing admiration for, and strong emotional response toward, the athletic boys in my class at school. My talents lay more in the intellectual sphere rather than with physical prowess. Since the former was not valued, I felt constantly inferior and longed to be like the boys I held in awe." Nothing overtly sexual in his account, more a desire to be liked and to belong.

Love First by Being Honest about Your Brokenness

I hope you've begun to see that, while some aspects of the SSA experience are unique, in many ways it's just like any other unwanted desire you or I might struggle with. SSA may get expressed differently, but some aspects of it map quite well onto everyday stories and challenges.

Do opposite-sex-attracted believers struggle with lust? Illicit thoughts? Pornography? Unmet expectations? Disappointing sexual experiences (within or outside of marriage)? Periods of sexual drought? If you're reading this as a person who experiences OSA, surely you understand. The OSA experience, which is no more uniform than the SSA experience, is not a smooth, mutually pleasing, guilt-free endeavor. It has its own set of struggles, temptations, and prevailing weaknesses. In that sense, SSA isn't so very different.

How can this kind of understanding lead us to deeper and more meaningful relationships with those who experience SSA? Any helpful answer to this question must include an emphasis on honest conversations. And here's some honesty that needs to enter into the conversation sooner rather than later: oftentimes the church, in seeking to contrast itself with the SSA experience, oversells the ease with which OSA people experience desire and intimacy. In an effort to uphold and extol God's original intention for sexuality, we talk about heterosexual intimacy in a way that glosses over our struggles and temptations.

When we talk with our friends who experience SSA, we shouldn't let this false picture stand. Let's talk in a way that reveals we all need the same thing: the grace of God to change our hearts, rearrange our expectations, and redeem our desires. Grace that meets us where we are but does not leave us as we are. Grace that realizes discipleship is a process not an instantaneous event.

With such seemingly diverse experiences, can we have unity in Christ without uniformity of experience? I believe the answer is a resounding, "Yes!" Why? We can have unity because of the gospel of Jesus Christ. The good news, that we are all sinners in need of God's grace, is the fundamental starting point for each and every one of us regardless of our life struggles.

While some might see this approach as a cop-out lending itself toward compromise, I believe it actually leads to an entirely different *goal*. When we move toward others who are in some ways different from us, we live out the basic premise of the gospel: a God who moves toward those he longs to redeem. Far from compromising our convictions, this approach puts our supreme conviction front and center: without the gospel we are—all of us—dead in our sins and wayward desires.

Will those who struggle with SSA discover the illuminating hope of the gospel through an abstract theological principle? Will they find it through political and ethical sloganeering? Or will they find it through personal relationship and lavish, redeeming grace? Rosaria Butterfield reflects on what her experience of Christians was like when, from the perspective of her openly lesbian lifestyle, she began to consider Christianity: "Even though obviously these Christians and I were very different, they seemed to know that I wasn't just a blank slate, that I had values and opinions too, and they talked with me in a way that didn't make me feel erased."[13]

Whether we are befriending Christians or non-Christians who experience SSA, may we strive to love them, not as if we want to erase their experience for our own convenience, but in a way that helps them see they are truly known and truly loved.

Four

GETTING TO KNOW A CHRISTIAN EXPERIENCING SSA

Key Markers on the Journey

"I don't feel like anyone knows the real me." All of us have felt this way at one time, and if we're honest, many of us have rarely felt otherwise. Lots of people know things *about* us—key life events, favorite jokes, hobbies, personality quirks—but that's not the same thing, is it? What is necessary for someone to know the real me?

At the risk of sounding too poetic or academic (and I may be guilty on both counts), knowing the real me requires understanding things like this:

- the overarching narrative that organizes the events of my life into a coherent whole
- the personal irony that makes certain jokes funny (at least to me)

- why I enjoy specific hobbies or pastimes
- the fears and passions that fuel my quirks

Until you know these things, all you know are things *about* me. That knowledge may allow you to effectively predict my behavior and anticipate my needs, but it is not what settles the troubled waters behind the truth, "It is not good that the man should be alone" (Genesis 2:18).

God is not satisfied when we can pass a theology quiz about him, and we are not satisfied when our friends can win a trivia game about us. We want someone to know the story of our lives in such a way that what moves us, moves them. We don't want to have to articulate the significance of everything that stirs our souls. We want to know that we can pick up in the middle of our stories and key points in the plot twist will still make sense.

How many people know you in this way? What would the loss of these relationships mean to you?

_____

_____

_____

_____

This chapter aims to help us get to know real people. It assumes you are a Christian who experiences opposite-sex attraction and that you are seeking to befriend a fellow Christian who is willing to trust you with his or her unwanted struggle with SSA. It will therefore focus on discipleship. (Looking ahead, the next chapter will focus primarily on befriending a non-Christian who experiences SSA, so the tone will be more evangelistic. But it's worth noting that, since both discipleship and evangelism are built on the same gospel foundation and both require relational capital to be effective, the two chapters are not as different as you might initially imagine.)

To help equip us, this chapter will cover two major themes:

- Understanding Key Markers on an SSA Journey
- How to Avoid Reducing a Person to Their Struggle

Understanding Key Markers on an SSA Journey

Imagine that you want to explain a favorite movie to someone. Basically, you could either summarize the plot—the key events—or you could present the main theme. In the case of *Braveheart*, for example, you could say, "William Wallace rallies a bunch of Scottish peasants to revolt and loses both his wife and life in the process," or you could take the theme approach and say, "It's about FREEDOM!!!" (in your best bloodcurdling Scottish warrior-poet voice).

If you have much of a conversation about the movie, you will wind up sharing both events and theme. But one will serve the other; either the events will be used to illustrate the theme, or the theme will be used to make sense of the events.

In this section we will look at five events or markers[14] common among those who experience SSA. Some of these are essential to SSA because they are part of the definition; others are neither necessary nor universal. All of them are worth understanding so that we can grasp the theme—the story or journey—of an actual person who experiences SSA. Here are two safeguards for employing the material in this section.

First, the point is not to address all these areas, or to address them in any particular order. For example, if your friend isn't ready to discuss number three, but does seem interested in talking about his or her "milestone of disclosure" (number four), that's fine. You don't need to understand any one area to have a valuable conversation about any other area. Observe simple conversational courtesy. Allow your friend to share in whatever order is natural and comfortable. Neither of you are bound to an outline.

Second, in any one area, don't view what follows as a checklist of questions that must be stepped through. This section, like the rest of this chapter, is meant to raise your personal awareness. The multiple bullet-point questions are intended to be illustrative, not required. It only takes one or two thoughtful questions to convey understanding and spark a meaningful conversation.

1. Initial Experience of SSA

Most of us can remember when we became romantically interested; the first person we "liked." There was a mixture of excitement and embarrassment. We wanted to tell somebody, but we didn't want anyone to know! This marker of social development is significant enough that most people can recall when it occurred.

The same is true for those who experience SSA—although the memorability of the experience is heightened by a sense of something being wrong. An analogy that may be helpful is that of expectant parents getting their first ultrasound, but it turns out there are complications. Whether the child is healthy or unhealthy, life is forever changing, but when something goes awry, the life-change is more pronounced and uncertain.

What kinds of questions can we ask to get to know this part of someone's story?

- When did you begin to experience SSA? What was your initial response to this sense of attraction?
- What messages had you heard about homosexuality? How did these impact your response to your sense of attraction?
- Did you know anyone you could talk to about it?
- How did this sense of attraction change your relationship with peers, parents, God, church, or others?
- What things were most hurtful or confusing for you at that time?
- What would have been most beneficial or comforting for you at that time?
- As your friend, what is most important for me to know about that season in your life?

What is gained from these conversations?

First, what does your friend gain? Your friend gains the opportunity to be known, the ability to share things that were hurtful and confusing, and the knowledge that somebody who knows them still wants to care for them.

Now, what do we gain? We gain the opportunity to be God's ambassadors to our friends. This is a high privilege. We don't have to know exactly what to say or do next in order to fulfill this calling—we can represent God well for a long time simply by caring enough to ask good questions and listen.

You can't unwrite history. You can't change the hurtful parts of your friend's story. But there are many good and helpful things you can do where it fits the circumstances.

- You might apologize on behalf of the church for Christians who have responded poorly.
- Expressing sympathy for the confusing years our SSA friend lived in silence might be comforting.
- Affirming areas of courage and wisdom in how they responded to a difficult experience at a young age could be encouraging.
- Identifying where unhealthy life patterns emerged (such as lying or living a double life) and helping them understand that these secrets are no longer needed in the context of your friendship might be instructive.
- Identifying how unhealthy beliefs emerged (e.g., *No one would love me if they knew*, or *If God were real he would take this away*) and engaging in conversations that lead to more redemptive beliefs could provide valuable insight.

We may also learn what reactions our SSA friends most fear from us. The hurt they've experienced in the past is likely the hurt they most fear in the future. There are many things we would like to promise but can't. We can't promise that if they take some specific set of actions (believe, pray, worship, study Scripture), then God will remove the experience of SSA. But we should be able to promise that *we* won't treat them in ways they have been needlessly hurt in the past.

2. Behavior in Response to SSA

While it can be awkward to talk about, it is true that attraction leads to behavior, and we need to be willing (if invited) to talk about behavior. We need to talk about it in this book, and at some point we will need to talk about it with our friends who struggle with SSA.

Imagine a boy in middle school experiencing SSA for the first time. The behavior that flows from his attraction may be as simple as sitting at a lunch table with a new romantic interest. It may be as risky as passing a note in class reading, "I like you. Do you like me? Yes No (circle one)." And it may express itself in experimenting with pornography and masturbation as a means of figuring out how his recently activated attraction-arousal system works.

Talking with someone about this part of his or her story requires the maturity to discuss the range of subjects I just mentioned. Later in this chapter we'll emphasize the fact that, while conversations about struggle and sexuality must not *define* the friendship, we can't simply avoid those subjects. To do so would be to demonstrate that we aren't ready to know "the real me."

What kinds of questions could we ask to get to know this part of someone's story?

- What did you do to try to change, offset, or satisfy your sense of attraction?
- How difficult was it for you to differentiate between same-gendered friends and romantic interests?
- Did you change friends, clothing style, music, heroes, or hobbies to try to live more authentically in light of your SSA?

- What emotions were dominant when you acted on SSA, and how did you (or do you) handle them?
- How did your relationship with God change with each of the things you attempted?

It would be easy for these conversations to create points of accountability or advice. If your friend desires this, be available and allow them to know areas where they can encourage or hold you accountable, too (that's what friends do). But *don't assume that if your friend offers information in these areas it amounts to an invitation to be held accountable.* For the time being, your friend may simply want to see how you respond or acclimate to such personal admissions.

What is gained from these conversations?

Your friend gains something very important—the ability to be known at another level. These are the type of disclosures that create the most shame, and about which we most fear being abandoned. We all live in fear that there is an unclear social line that will render us "unfriendable." In these kinds of conversations we know that, if such a line does exist, we're probably getting close to it.

In seeking to serve our friends who experience SSA, one of our goals must be to communicate and demonstrate, through our presence and our compassion, that for God and God's people, no such line of banishment exists. Thanks to Christ's purchase of forgiveness, behavior *in and of itself* can never constitute grounds for outright rejection. The risk factor for God's rejection is not primarily our sin but our attitude toward our sin. The refusal to repent—in effect, to insist that our sin is more satisfying than God—can be grounds for church discipline (see Matthew 18) and is a very dangerous place before God. Notice, however, that those who will trust us by voluntarily disclosing their struggles with SSA are demonstrating that they are not simply rejecting biblical teaching about sin.[15]

After you have a conversation about behaviors emerging from SSA, consider saying something like this: "I really appreciate how honest you're willing to be with me. It shows a great deal of trust in our friendship, and I'm honored and humbled by that. When I hear tangible expressions of how someone is struggling, my tendency is to try to make it better. I'm not sure what that would look like and realize that may not be want you want. What would be the most helpful way for me to follow up on our conversation?"

Your friend may have a practical suggestion you hadn't thought of. Or again, what might be most encouraging for your friend at this point is for both of you to simply take some time to get used to this new level of shared understanding. If that's the case, tell him or her that you value the friendship and that you want to continue being a supportive friend as the two of you learn what it means for each of you to follow God.

3. The Question of Identity

Whatever we are most drawn to is what we tend to become. Whether a sport, a hobby, a career, a social role, an art form, a cause, a person, a lifestyle—if we are attracted to it we tend take on its characteristics or the characteristics of others who value it. This is true even if the attraction is grounded in sins we would much rather be free from (see Romans 7).

The experience of SSA is no different. Imagine a middle schooler facing questions like: *What does it mean for my mind and body to respond to the same sex in ways I thought it would respond to the opposite sex? How much of my life does this explain and impact?* This is deep and complex territory, challenging even for philosophers and psychologists. No wonder young people experiencing SSA are confused! Yet the answers they reach in middle school—often with little or no helpful counsel—form the conclusions they draw as high schoolers, dictating the choices they make in their late teens and 20s. This is why the church cannot be silent. And it is why, as the church, we must give at least as much (if not more) attention to speaking in private circles of personal friendship as we do in the public square of open debate.

I believe that discipleship is more a matter of identity formation than of behavior modification or even the head knowledge of mere doctrinal education. If this is true, then local churches should be well-versed in having honest conversations about those areas that have the largest impact on our identity.

What kinds of questions could we ask to get to know this part of someone's story?

- Which features of your personality do you attribute to the experience of SSA?
- Which of your personal interests do you attribute to the experience of SSA?
- Which of your personal struggles do you attribute to the experience of SSA?
- What groups of people or activities do you avoid because of your experience of SSA?

- When was the first time you thought, *Am I gay?* and, *What would it mean if I am?*
- What forms of relief or opportunity would come with embracing a gay identity?
- What costs or limitations would come with embracing a gay identity?
- What are the sources of pressure you feel to identify a certain way?
- In this process, who do you trust to be most for *you* as opposed to being for their own position?

What is gained from these conversations?

We gain an appreciation for the weight of decision that the experience of SSA introduces to someone's life at an early age. Knowing that you grasp, to some degree, the mental-emotional task your friend has been grappling with since puberty can be an immense relief for your friend. Asking questions that allow your friend to tell his or her story—rather than giving quick solutions or judgments—is liberating. Not liberating from the experience of SSA but from the turmoil of being misunderstood that often surrounds it.

These conversations can help your friend understand how SSA is often seen, erroneously, as explaining nearly everything about a person. I had a friend who once said, "I like tennis, cooking, and walks on the beach. What else can it mean, but I'm gay?!?" The abruptness of his comment meant we were in danger of moving from conversation to debate. However, because I knew him fairly well, I realized that this kind of direct banter was part of his normal, endearing communication style. Also, his body language and tone of voice indicated that he still felt safe. But the comment itself revealed a great deal. For him, the experience of SSA was becoming much more central to his identity—so much so that now certain sports, hobbies, and indeed the entire field of culinary arts had become non-heterosexual.

Obviously none of these things, separately or in combination, belong to either gender or any sexual orientation. SSA does not explain such interests, and such interests do not point to SSA. Do people with opposite-sex attraction engage in (pick a hobby, a sport, or any interest that's not sexual in nature) because they are heterosexual?

By ascribing excessive explanatory power to SSA, my friend was sabotaging his own desire to resist it. This was something we needed to talk about as friends—not to challenge his experience of SSA or try to decrease his attractions but to comfort his pain without affirming his over-generalized conclusion. In his case, excess emotion, generalization, and jumping to conclusions had disrupted many of his relationships. This too he saw as a sign of being gay.[16] SSA, for him, had come to explain nearly everything else about him. This was both erroneous and harmful.

4. The Milestone of Disclosure

Think back to big disclosures in your life—perhaps admitting to a parent or teacher that you had lied or cheated; saying to a significant other for the first time, "I love you;" or (if you come from a non-Christian home) telling your parents you have become a follower of Christ. These moments are markers in your life. And unless you come from a Muslim background, where a profession of Christianity could jeopardize your family relationships, the disclosures you've made have likely been of far less emotional and social consequence than acknowledging the experience of SSA.

SSA disclosures come in at least two types: private acknowledgment of a personal struggle or public identification as gay. Tragically, because of widespread misunderstanding about the distinction between same-sex attraction and gay identity (as we discussed in chapter two), people often feel they must hide their SSA until they have the courage to "come out."

The kind of friendship advocated for in this book can be an ideal context for earlier SSA disclosure. Indeed, one of my great hopes for this book is that it will help cultivate contexts in which SSA disclosures can be made sooner, before someone feels forced to identify openly as gay in an effort to gain some relief from the internal tension. (At these earlier points, conversations are less likely to turn into debates.) The local church can—indeed, must—become a safe place in which to acknowledge the struggle of SSA. Only then will Christians who experience SSA have something God intends for every believer: a community of support in which to process their own experience of suffering and temptation.

When someone who experiences SSA or has embraced a gay identity begins to disclose that to us, what kinds of questions could we ask to get to know this part of his or her story?

- Have you confided in anyone else about your experience of SSA? If so, how did that person respond?
- What are the most important things I could do to help these conversations feel safe for you?

- What are you afraid I will think or do as you share this information with me?
- What form of relief do you want to gain by letting others know what you're experiencing?

What is gained from these conversations?

Your friend can gain a sense of safety. Disclosure is a time when people quickly recognize which individuals and communities are safe for them. Here the adage, "You never get a second chance to make a first impression," is especially true.

Keep in mind that the two of you are at very different places with respect to this journey your friend is on. For you, the disclosure is the very beginning; for your friend it is just the latest step in an already long road. For you, the disclosure introduces a brand new tension and may seem premature or hasty. To your friend, it is a *release* of tension, one that probably feels overdue.

If you're not alert to these realities, they can harm communication. So remember that the disclosure and subsequent conversations are not about you and your reactions to this news. Whenever we are uncomfortable or insecure, we tend to become more self-centered. But the focus here should be on your friend, not yourself. Remain other-minded. The important question is not, "What is it like for me to receive this information?" It is, "What is it like for my friend to talk to me, and how can I best demonstrate care or provide support?"

5. The Establishment of a Same-Sex Relationship

The culmination of disclosure, at least for those who are

considering embracing a gay identity, is having a same-sex romantic relationship. This is when it can get especially awkward for Christians and social conservatives. Suddenly it is easy to think that if we continue to maintain the friendship, to be kind and compassionate, we have compromised our values by tacitly condoning a sinful relationship.

But it bears repeating that cutting ties, turning away, or becoming offended when people choose to believe or live in a manner contrary to Scripture is not a Christian response. We are called to love our fellow believers (John 13:34-35), our neighbors (Mark 12:31), and even our enemies (Matthew 5:44). Surely this list encompasses those who have embraced a gay identity. By this point in the book I hope you have begun to see that as a rule those who experience SSA are not enemies but at least neighbors if not fellow believers.

When someone we know is in a romantic same-sex relationship, what kinds of questions could we ask to get to know that part of the person's story?

- How did the two of you meet?
- How long have you been together?
- How have people—family, friends, Christians—responded to your relationship?
- What are some of the dumb things people say when they learn about your relationship? I would prefer to learn from their mistakes than risk making them myself.
- *If your friends have children*: How do your kids refer to each of you? (Use those titles when referencing a given parent to one of the children.)

- Would the two of you like to come over for dinner?
- What do the two of you do for fun? Could I/we join you?

What is gained from these conversations?

You gain an opportunity for ongoing godly influence, which is good for both of you. The point of this section echoes a core theme of the book: regardless of how your friend is responding to his or her experience of SSA, relationship is a primary means by which God works in our lives. If you're unwilling to develop relationship, then telling someone how to live is perceived as offensive — because it is.

In the course of building a friendship, therefore, you should always strive to be openly Christian. As you do, conversations will inevitably include various issues related to the political topics of the day, including what the Bible says about homosexuality. The quality of your friendship will determine the tone of these conversations.

Friends can disagree with one another and still respect each other's differences; acquaintances feel much more pressure to persuade each other. Chances are your friend will ask many questions and make many points that impact how you think about SSA and homosexuality. That's okay. Genuine friendships always have mutual influence. If we aren't open to this, we aren't open to being a friend. Staying connected with other Christian friends who can encourage and support you as you authentically wrestle with these difficult questions is important.

Again, it is vital to remember that in these conversations it is not your job to convince or change anyone. Your only goal is to represent Christ well and speak truth in the context of love—a mutually valued friendship. If that is accomplished, you've done all that God has asked.

How to Avoid Reducing a Person to Their Struggle

In this book, as in the conversations I hope this book creates, we will have to strive continually to ensure that the subject of SSA does not become more important than the person who experiences it. With that in mind, I would like to offer three thoughts on how to avoid reducing a person to his or her struggle.

1. **Have fun together.** Mutual enjoyment is a good indicator that a friendship is not devolving into a project relationship. Mutual enjoyment builds memories and stories. Mutual enjoyment strengthens the relationship. And the stronger the relationship is, the less likely either of you will be to give offense or take offense. What the fun looks like will vary in every friendship, but try to see the fun for what it is— the mortar between the bricks rather than merely the icing on the cake.

2. **Go broad, not narrow.** If SSA is the majority topic of conversation, your relationship will become more therapeutic or polemical than friendly. So spend the majority of your time talking about subjects other than SSA. This is how you make the friendship about life and shared interests not about SSA as such. For example, if the two of you have this kind of discipleship relationship, study a book of the Bible together or a mutually relevant Christian book. Seek what God says about all of life together not just SSA.

3. **Allow your friend to speak into your life as well.**
   The most effective way to gain the right to be heard
   is to listen. Particularly if your friend is a Christian,
   they have something to offer you. Even if they're not,
   they have a life experience that is different from yours
   and can offer a fresh perspective. Much can be learned
   about how someone thinks by asking, "How do you
   see my situation? What would you do and why?"
   Asking these kinds of questions will likely bless you
   and advance the friendship you want to build.

   Again, please remember that this chapter is meant
   to help you build friendship not to serve as a checklist or
   manual. If you feel like you can now ask a caring question
   when, prior to reading this chapter you would have been
   silent, you've gotten everything this chapter can offer.
   From there, just be a good friend. Laugh in the good times,
   listen well in the hard times, and allow your friend to
   invest as much in you as you do in him or her.

Five

GETTING TO KNOW A NON-CHRISTIAN EXPERIENCING SSA

Winning an Argument vs. Influencing a Friend

Debate has a valuable place—just not as a way to build friendship. Debates tend to entrench positions and usually result in each person being even more committed to their original view. So if our goal is godly influence through genuine friendship, we must learn how to keep conversations about SSA or homosexuality from turning into debates.

What's the difference between a safe-but-hard conversation and an argument or debate? In a word, trust. When we believe the other person is for us, we are generally willing to hear hard things. When we think the other person might be against us, even mildly unpleasant things are often received as an attack. Even in healthy marriages where there is little doubt about each other's love and commitment, when trust temporarily dissipates, conversations quickly become arguments.

That's why this chapter is designed to help your conversations remain conversations. In chapter four my predominant assumption was that you were talking with a Christian who struggled with SSA. In this chapter most of the focus will be on how to have conversations with non-Christians who experience SSA, conversations that we pray will lead to the gospel.

For now, don't brace yourself for those what-do-I-say-when moments. The better you become at applying the material from the first five chapters of this book, the stronger the relational bridge of trust will be when you have to pass over those waters. Getting *to* difficult conversations well is often the biggest part of navigating those conversations effectively. In fact, if conversational entry points aren't available, don't press it. Eventually life compels us all to reach out to those we trust. Continue to be an openly Christian friend. The better friend you are, the shorter this time will be.

Same Topic, Different Conversations

We've all had the experience, talking about the same subject but having different conversations. Maybe it's discussing a job change with a friend where he is focused on the financial benefits, while you are weighing questions of personal fulfillment. Or it could be a political topic where you're weighing the principle of justice, but your friend is concerned about unintended consequences.

We all know this happens, and when it does the outcome is either confusion or hurt feelings. I want to help you see *how* this happens in conversations on any subject. Here are four levels at which a topic can be discussed.

1. **Facts** – What is true about the situation?
2. **Definitions** – How should the key concepts be defined or labeled?
3. **Values** – How should we weigh the importance of key factors that are in conflict?
4. **Action Steps** – What should we do or believe?

To help you acclimate to these categories, let's use the example of a husband and wife trying to decide whether to paint a bathroom in their home.

1. **Facts** – How much can we afford to spend? What can be done for that much money? How much longer do we plan to be in this home?
2. **Definitions** – Is this a *want* or *need* project?
3. **Values** – "If we paint it that weekend, I would have to cancel my golf tournament." Or, "If we wait until after that weekend, the girls coming over for the baby shower won't get to see it."
4. **Action Steps** – Who is going to do the painting? What color do we choose? Stripes?!?

It's important to recognize the differences between these levels, because when our questions bridge or combine levels we usually end up with loaded questions that easily create friction. Here are two examples. She: "If we hope to be in this house for 10 more years (fact), isn't that worth you canceling a golf tournament (value)?" He:

"But if painting this bathroom is only a *want* and not a *need* (definition), isn't my having community with other men and getting exercise more important (value)?"

Do you see how these end up as loaded or even unfair questions? Whoever is asking the question tends to stack up a strong "good" against the other person's point of resistance, in a way that ultimately amounts to an apples-to-oranges comparison. This seems fair to the one person until the other person asks an equally loaded question, at which point the other person is "obviously" being unreasonable. How many marriages have gotten lost in the labyrinth of regularly trying to navigate these kinds of disconnected debates?

This brings us to a key distinction between conversations vs. debates or arguments:

- In a *conversation* our aim is to honor one another and cooperate for mutual benefit. Therefore we pay attention to categories (even if unconsciously) and overtly shift between them with a certain amount of care, to keep the conversation on track.
- In a *debate* our aim is to win, so we generally dishonor one another, even if unintentionally. We may believe our view of things would also be best for the other person, but because we see their view as wrong, we are far more inclined to covertly bridge and combine categories as a way of gaining leverage, forcing the dialogue in a direction that gives us an advantage.

As sinners, we fall into debate mode quite naturally. Indeed, we are all highly skilled manipulators with motives that are often far from pure. If at any point a conversation begins to feel like a game of intellectual chess, it has become a debate.

My goal for you by the end of this chapter is to be able to identify the level at which conversation is being had, so that you can determine the most Christ-honoring, gospel-relevant way to have that conversation. The chart below is intended as a tool to help you think through the relevance of these categories, the goal being fruitful conversations about SSA. The topics listed are merely representative and not exhaustive. The chart is meant to ensure that both of you are having the same conversation on the same subject.

The left column of the chart (which is not being advocated as fruitful) helps you understand what debate looks like in the context of SSA. These topics and approaches are more "debate material" because they tend to frame the conversation in a way that suggests the topic is more important than the person, or that change should be easy after a certain insight is attained.[17] The right column should seem familiar, since much of it echoes ideas developed earlier in this book.

	Debate-Oriented Focal Points	Conversation-Oriented Focal Points
Facts	• Research on genetic studies • Historic correlations to societies where homosexuality was accepted • Injustices resulting from religious and civil law being too tightly correlated	• Tell me about your experience of sexual attraction and people's responses (chapters two, three, and four material). • What have your conversations with Christians been like? • *Do we believe God is our creator and the designer of all things, including sexuality?*
Definitions	• Insisting on the use of SSA, GI, and HB language in conversation • Appealing to experts' or theologians' definitions of particular terms or concepts • Creating a straw man version of each other's views	• How are we using key terms or concepts (chapters one and five material)? • Why are these words important to us? • *Do we believe God's definition of "good" for something is often different from our natural preferences?*

Values	• Creating slippery-slope arguments • "That means you also have to believe…" • "Isn't it better for a child to have a mother and a father instead of two of one?" or "Isn't it better for a child to have some family even if you think same-sex parents are undesirable?"	• What weighs most heavily in your thinking about SSA? • What would be most disappointing or scary if each of us were wrong? • *Are we willing to trust that God will care for us on our journey in following him?*
Action Steps	• Telling someone what they should do with their life or what they should believe • "If you don't repent you're going to hell." • "If you don't morally agree with my lifestyle you're a bigot."	• What is the wisest thing to do when we're uncertain about a situation? • How are either of us currently acting in ways that are outside of or beyond what we know to be true or good? • *Are you willing to place your faith in God and trust him with your life?*

In a moment we will take some time to look at how to have redemptive conversations at each of these four levels. But first, a few general comments about how to use this grid.

First, be willing to engage at whatever level your friend wants to talk. Don't think your conversations have to step through this grid—or any system—block-by-block. Projects are about following a system, but friendship is not. You will either arrive at the gospel implications of SSA or homosexuality in a way that feels natural and conversational, or you will push your friend away from those implications by making the conversation operate within artificial constraints.

Second, don't try to gain a deeper theological commitment than what your friend currently has. This is about the italicized sections at the bottom of each right-column block. In this case, it actually *is* wise to keep the order of the blocks in mind. For example, if your friend hasn't embraced the theology represented by the italicized language in the Facts and Definitions boxes, it's not wise to address the theology found in the italicized language in the Values box. You'll either come off as offensive or the two of you will be speaking past each other about what "trusting God to care for us" means. Either way, this will probably just produce a premature impasse. Remember, if SSA and homosexuality comprise the majority of your conversations, you are probably allowing your friendship to devolve into a debate.

Third, speak in third-person plural (i.e., we, us) whenever possible. Notice that the gospel conversations in this book are worded in mutual language. *We* all need the gospel every day, whether it is our initial need for justification or our ongoing need for sanctification. Those who experience SSA do not need the gospel in a special way, nor do they need the gospel-on-steroids. Everyone's need for the gospel is the same. We want to model the daily reliance upon the gospel that we're inviting our friend into. For many readers, it will be most effective to keep in mind the simple truth that *we are all sinners in need of the same grace*. This will help guide conversations until the friendship develops to the point that overtly Christian themes can emerge in the dialogue.

Too often we think of gospel conversations only as appeals to salvation. If you read this chapter through that lens, you could easily assume that the presence of SSA means the absence of saving faith. This is obviously not necessarily true. When we assume, without engaging in these kinds of conversations, that people who struggle with SSA are not believers, we do more harm than good.

Level One: Facts

This is the most contentious level at which people can disagree. Regardless of the subject, when people disagree over what they see as matters of fact, both sides immediately assume the other person is spiritually blind, misinformed, lying, hateful, or evil. In any event, we see the other person's position as having no merit, and we probably believe they need teaching, correction, and/or condemnation.

To complicate matters further, whatever one may believe about SSA, the subject is often seen as more clear-cut and factual than it really is. Perceived "facts" about SSA can include the clarity of genetic research findings and theories or stereotypes about, for example, the role of an absent father, childhood sexual abuse, or non-gender-stereotypical interests in its formation.

In our conversations, we must never assume that understanding the latest thinking about a subject is equivalent to knowing a person; theories can get in the way of learning about actual individuals. The principal danger with theories and stereotypes is that they easily mistake possibilities for facts. Consider that, even if a stereotype is 70 percent true (a dangerous assumption), then 30 percent of the time it's still 100 percent false.

Imagine you are talking to your friend who experiences SSA and you bring up a theory about SSA formation. If it applies to him or her, all you've done is turn your friend into a statistic, a caricature. You've created potential grounds for an offense while establishing nothing that's actually helpful.

Or what if you could show your friend that the research claiming to demonstrate a genetic basis for homosexuality showed strong sampling biases? What is the likelihood that their response would be, "Well, if the research is flawed, I must not be experiencing SSA!" That's right, at the individual level it wouldn't matter. Probably the only thing you could ever accomplish by debating research studies would be to demonstrate that you're more interested in defending your position than in knowing the person.

Therefore, the facts initially most worth discussing in SSA conversations are the factual experiences of your friend. Regardless of the moral weight we place on these experiences, they are a reality we must understand if we are to merit the high title of "friend."

There are names for so-called advice from people

who don't know us and our particular situation: clichés and platitudes.[18] On the other hand, input from someone who knows us well is almost always received as being of higher value and relevance. When we honestly care about getting to know our friend's experience, our conversation can attain to the standard of Proverbs 25:11, "A word fitly spoken is like apples of gold in a setting of silver."

As part of your conversation, however, a key gospel fact certainly worth discussing is the reality of God as creator—and the clear implication that creation, therefore, has a designed intent. With respect to SSA, here are the options:

1. God has no created intention for sexuality, or if he does, it includes SSA.
2. God does have a created intention for sexuality, and it does not include SSA.

If the first option is true, then the gospel is only relevant to SSA in the same way it is relevant to a career choice or how many children a couple has. But if the second option is true, then SSA is a product of the fall. Like so many other areas of human nature, it represents a diversion from a natural disposition to one that is unnatural.[19] Unwanted SSA is therefore a "dispositional brokenness" much like many of the compulsive, addictive, and depressive tendencies that cause so much disruption to individuals, families, and society.

Level Two: Definitions
Language is never neutral. The more difficult the conversation, the more important this point becomes. When

people disagree about what words mean or which words should be used when discussing a particular topic, there are three options:

1. Promote your preferred terminology, usually by casting the worst-case-scenario meaning on the other person's preference.
2. Stop the conversation, which usually results in a feeling of self-justification when you tell yourself the other person was being unreasonable.
3. Seek to understand the purpose behind your friend's preferred terminology and honor that preference. This means representing it fairly in tone and content, even if you disagree with it. This usually feels uncomfortable and slows down the conversation—and that's a good thing.

For example, what goes through your mind when you hear the phrase, "gay Christian"? If you are intent on being a good friend, you need to try to understand what the other person is saying. There are at least four possibilities.

1. A gay Christian is (or the definition can include) someone who believes the central tenets of the gospel,[20] experiences ongoing SSA, does not intend to pursue same-sex romantic interests, but wants to avoid suggesting that either their possession of faith or their diligent practice of the faith has changed their sense of attraction, because at least at this point it hasn't.
2. A gay Christian is (or the definition can include) someone who believes the central tenets of the

gospel, is engaged in a same-sex romantic relationship, believes this choice is wrong, but does not want
to renounce his or her faith, all of which produce a
conflict of conscience.

3. A gay Christian is (or the definition can include)
someone who believes the central tenets of the gospel,
is engaged in a same-sex romantic relationship, but
does not believe that committed SSA relationships
are wrong, and therefore does not experience a
conflict of conscience.

4. There are no gay Christians. It is an inherently
contradictory phrase because each word negates
the possibility of the other, like "hot snow" or "dry
water."

If you and your friend mean different things by "gay
Christian" and don't realize it, your communication will
be muddled at best. Moreover, if you can't agree to use
the same definition, it's not likely you will be able to forge
a true friendship or keep talking honestly and construc-
tively. After all, when two people disagree on a theological
concept, they both think God is on their side. This creates
nothing less than a relational minefield: "If you disagree
with me, you disagree with God."

What, therefore, is a conservative Christian to do if he
or she, in the name of moving the friendship forward, has
to (in this example) use "gay Christian" in conversation
in a way that seems wrong or unhelpful? In other words,
what does it mean to honor the other person's terminology without agreeing with their definition?

The answer lies in understanding and taking on the
role of an ambassador. We are ambassadors of Christ (2

Corinthians 5:20), and central to the role of any good ambassador is understanding the beliefs and positions of the culture or people to which he or she has been assigned. To understand what someone else means by a specific term and to allow that meaning to stand *in the limited context of conversation with them*, is not a denial of real truth, but an act of compassion and kindness. And it is done in the hope that it will ultimately help build a gospel-centered friendship.

Imagine that your friend self-identifies as a "gay Christian" using the first definition. You can affirm him or her for not wanting to imply that faith has simply swept away the SSA. But you could also suggest that you believe it's not best to use a self-descriptive phrase that centers one's identity on a sense of attraction. Then, you could *understand* that particular use of "gay Christian" without advocating its use by others.

In other instances, definitional differences may center on truly significant theological issues, such as in the third definition above, which to me cannot be reconciled with Scripture. Such differences need to become ongoing points of careful, compassionate conversation. Indeed, they likely reveal a disconnect at the level of Facts—specifically God as creator and his design for sexuality—and therefore need to be engaged with at that level before a theological commitment at the Definitions level is even possible.

This is why gospel conversations at the Definitions level ultimately must focus on the last element in that box: whether God, as creator, gets to define the acceptable and unacceptable uses of everything he has made, including sex. Agreement here is the prerequisite for productive conversation at the Values and Actions levels.

Lastly on this point, don't go into Definitions conversations assuming that your friend who experiences SSA will disagree with your preferred terminology. Many in our local churches and communities experience unwanted SSA and aren't sure what to do or who they can talk to. If the Christians they know are primarily debate-oriented, then the only *conversational* outlet for them will be the gay community. But conversations that are handled with honor can often move to level three (Values) with little resistance and much appreciation as trust and friendship grow.

Level Three: Values

Isn't X more important than Y? This is a harder question than we often think—especially if someone is torn between choosing one or the other.

"Isn't honoring God more important than your sex life?" "Isn't personal fulfillment more important than sexual ethics?" If we say X is better, it can feel like we're saying Y has no value at all. If we promote Y, it's as if we don't care about X. Can you feel the tension?

In the church, the subject of inappropriate sexuality has an unusual tendency to cause the human factor to fade to the background. Not everyone who struggles with sexual temptation is callously and casually disregarding God. In our rush to insist on X or Y, the person who struggles between the two tends to vanish.

This is why I believe that having conversations that hover around simplistic X vs. Y questions are rarely a good way forward. This is especially true in the case of someone who wants to do the right thing but is confused and emotionally torn. With someone like this, getting to the "right" answer requires an approach that is far less direct—but also far more loving and far more likely to succeed.

The constructive alternative to an X vs. Y question is something like this: "What weighs most heavily in your thinking about SSA?" This approach positions you to cover the same conversational ground while building and affirming the relationship. By contrast, X vs. Y questions tend to neglect and weaken the relationship by minimizing the struggles of the very person you want to befriend.

Do you see the irony here? In the name of befriending someone because they are struggling between X and Y, an insistence on X or Y minimizes the difficulty of their struggle. At that point, it looks as though your goal is not primarily to care for a person you like but to fix a problem you don't like.

So don't be a mechanic, an engineer, or a morality cop. Be a friend. It is not a compromise of biblical truth to resonate with the emotional sacrifice of obedience. In fact, chances are that what weighs most heavily on your friend is not sexual frustration but loneliness. Is there anyone who can't genuinely empathize with loneliness? If you can, and you communicate that, you are already offsetting its impact.

Ministry is always incarnational. Jesus took on flesh, got hungry, felt fatigue, experienced disease, and was tempted in every way that we are. He didn't have to expose himself to these struggles. He did it as a way of reaching us—so we can know he understands every obstacle that would cause us to doubt his love (Hebrews 2:14-18, 4:14-16). Likewise, friendship is incarnational ministry. We genuinely enter the turmoil of another's dilemma so that every obstacle to trust Christ is faced side-by-side with a compassionate member of the body of Christ, the church.

Here's a statement you may find challenging: you should not be able to have these value-level conversations with a friend who experiences unwanted SSA and avoid tears, or at least deep and genuine sadness (Romans 12:15). We should have no joy in merely "being right." *Our joy is in who God is for us,* not in the positions we take on his behalf in a broken world.

At the Value level, then, the ultimate goal of our conversation is a gospel question: do we have faith in God's willingness and ability to provide what we need? To your friend, this translates as: can John 10:10—a full life in Christ—be true for me, as someone who experiences SSA, if I commit to Christ?

This is huge: probably the ultimate question. In all your conversations, this will likely be the largest crisis-point of faith for your friend. The godly relationship you've forged up to this point will be absolutely vital to your friend being able to respond with a believable *yes*. For that to happen—for that *yes* to be more than mere wishing and sentimentality—the family of God must have become to your friend more than an appealing theological concept. It must have been experienced as a reality (Ephesians 2:17-22).

Level Four: Action Steps

This level usually represents the most straightforward part of the journey, although not necessarily the easiest. If you have moved well through levels one through three, the outlook for level four is bright. At this point, the steps for you and your friend (remember, we're trying to use "we" language) are clear: Embrace the gospel in *saving* faith or continue to embrace the gospel in *sustaining* faith. This we must all do daily. How?

- By confiding in Christian friends for love and support
- By taking refuge in God's grace for all of life's struggles
- By resisting lust in whatever form it may take (i.e., sexual, financial, social, power, etc.)
- By never pretending to be stronger than you are and thereby foregoing the care of others or forfeiting God's provision
- By longing with eager patience for the full redemption of all things
- By making wise decisions inside God's will day-by-day

For someone who has historically experienced SSA, what does this point in the conversation mean for potential opposite-sex dating or marriage? Again, that will vary. The level of elasticity in one's attractions can differ significantly from one person to another, especially after removing the living-with-secrets dynamic. But here are a few guidelines if dating is something your friend wants to consider.

- Don't view opposite-sex marriage as the answer to same-sex attraction.
- Don't use dating as a litmus test to see "if anything has changed."

- Feel the freedom to date if you're genuinely interested in someone of the opposite sex.
- Begin disclosing your experience of SSA at the transition from casual to serious dating.
- Realize you can be a great spouse with a moderate sense of sexual attraction.
- Allow the leading question to be, "Can we see ourselves enjoying life serving one another in a lifelong romantic friendship?"

Remember also that celibacy is not failure. It is, rather, the gift for which few volunteer. In a given local church, the better we do at being the family of God, the less that celibacy will be equated with isolation and loneliness, or being unknown and unloved. We cannot predict how someone's sexual desires will be affected by the experience of being fully known and fully loved by God and his people. But we can give them reason to believe that, regardless, they will be well cared for.

Conclusion

A final point of clarification should be made. As Christians, we must honor the right of our friend to take a break or walk away from these conversations—whether a particular conversation or the dialogue as a whole. If we press a conversation longer than our friend willingly participates, we are not just perceived as offensive; we are being offensive. The closer the relationship, the more difficult this juncture may be. For example, honoring disengagement from a conversation by a son or daughter is much harder than when it's a classmate or colleague.

Remember, it is never our role to change anybody—

not their sexual orientation, not their personal beliefs. However noble or sincere we may believe our motives to be, it is wrong to try to do this. You and I cannot change anyone, and we must not act or pretend otherwise. Our role is as ambassadors of a message. We want to share and embody the gospel while showing genuine interest in a friendship, and then to honor the freedom of the other individual to respond as they see fit.

This reiterates one of my central points: *this book is not a strategy manual*. Rather, it's intended to give you a base of understanding you can apply in a wide variety of situations. After all, you don't know what role God may have you play in any individual's life. Perhaps you are their first exposure to an understanding Christian. Perhaps you plant the first seed explaining the gospel. Maybe you see them come to faith, or walk with them for an important leg in their journey. Maybe you'll be a meaningful memory; someone they recall as a caring person who helped draw them back to considering Christianity. Or maybe you'll be a lifelong friend who walks with them through so many of life's ups and downs.

Be content to be a good ambassador-friend. Fill that role for as long as they allow. Trust God with how he chooses to use your influence in their life, and learn as much from the entire experience as you can. That is the difference between winning a debate and influencing a friend.

Six

NAVIGATING DIFFICULT CONVERSATIONS

If you're flipping to this chapter first in the hope of finding some handy takeaways, I strongly encourage you to go back and start at the beginning. This is not a book about quick-fix solutions or silver-bullet answers. In fact, in the absence of quality relationships, merely offering the "right answers" to difficult questions involving SSA nearly always does more harm than good. That's one reason why the style of this chapter is predominantly conversational rather than a catalog of Q&A responses. Before getting into the conversation format, let's look briefly at two subjects.

<u>How do I avoid sabotaging a conversation before it starts?</u> I trust that these points will feel like fairly obvious extensions of what you have read in the previous chapters.

- *Avoid crude humor about homosexuality.* In general, Christians should abstain from humor on any topic that is rooted in shaming or mocking others. This falls short of God's command, "So whatever you wish that others would do to you, do also to them, for this is the Law and the Prophets" (Matthew 7:12).

- *Avoid utilizing stereotypes about the gay community.* Utilizing stereotypes demonstrates laziness in our professed willingness to get to know people for who they really are. In the eyes of someone who experiences SSA, such laziness is very likely to disqualify you as a safe person to talk to.
- *Be careful how you characterize political positions.* How you present the position you are against is at least as important as how you present the position you are for. To be trustworthy, you must represent fairly those you disagree with, neither vilifying them nor suggesting they are unworthy of compassion and understanding.

How do I actually start the conversation? If you picked up this book because you already have a friend confiding their experience of SSA to you, this question is not a problem. But if you started reading this book out of a general desire to see the church more effectively engage its gay neighbors as well as its members who experience SSA, admittedly this may be the most difficult part.

- *Don't "out" the person.* It is unwise to put someone on the spot with a question like, "Are you gay?" Even if you think you know, respect this person's right to disclose the information on their timetable. Nobody wants to live with a secret. If you prove yourself to be a safe person, they will want to talk sooner rather than later.
- *Speak sympathetically to the struggle of SSA.* Humble

statements can go a long way. "I can only imagine how hard it would be to experience unwanted same-sex attraction and feel caught in so many cultural debates. Trying to figure out who to talk to might be as hard as anything else. That would be incredibly lonely." A statement like this in social contexts where homosexuality is being discussed raises a flag of peace to be seen by those looking for a safe friend.

- *Study this book with your small group.* It may work best to first equip existing friends within your church. A small group that has learned to be a safe place for SSA conversations is an excellent beginning for a church and an ideal place to invite someone who may experience SSA. It can give your friend a chance to see that your church may actually offer real community.

A Difficult Conversation Handled Well

For the remainder of this chapter we are going to envision a dialogue between you and a gay-identifying non-Christian who, in this scenario, poses relatively antagonistic questions. (For the sake of simplicity, I'm going to portray your friend as male.) Allow me to explain why I have taken this approach.

I am not doing it to typecast those who identify as gay as aggressive. I am simply offering a model of how to navigate more-difficult moments. Should such moments arise in your own conversations, this guidance may help prevent them from needlessly damaging the friendship.

I am not implying that Christians never experience SSA. I trust this is clear from all I have said previously in this book. Instead, I am imagining your friend as a non-Christian in order to set out a conversation with a wider belief gap.

I am not suggesting that conversations often move as quickly as the one set forth below. This is a highly compressed dialogue offered for illustrative purposes. It's difficult to imagine this kind of pace in a real-world context.

The "you" language may not sound like you. But that's not really the point. It's the overall approach that's important. So don't let any mismatch put you off. In fact, use each exchange to ask yourself, "How would I respond?" As you critique my dialogue, put it in your own voice. Do a lot of writing in the margins (or the digital equivalent if you're not using a paperback). The italicized comments are meant to help you think and write more clearly.

Let's get started.

* * *

Your Friend: You're a Christian but you're nicer than I expected. I can't figure out where you're at on the homosexuality debate that came up in our last class/meeting. If I told you I was gay, what would you think of me?

You: Thank you. I regret that the public discourse is so tense that it would be surprising for you to meet a "nice Christian." I try not to get lost in subjects or debates. My goal is to love God and love people well regardless of the subject. As for my opinion of you, I would admire your courage for asking, appreciate your trust in asking me, and your grace for giving me the benefit of the doubt.

Look for things to affirm early. Even in an introduc-

tion more antagonistic than this one you could say, "I appreciate you sharing with me things that are very important to you. Silence can create as much division as harsh interactions. I hope our conversation can avoid both of those outcomes."

Friend: Well, then I'll tell you. I *am* gay. And, honestly, you didn't answer my real question. Do you think it's wrong for me to be gay? If we become friends, will you try to "convert" me and help me become straight so I won't be "living in sin" anymore?

You: I appreciate you letting me know your real question and wanting to know my thoughts. I don't think either of us would be satisfied trying to summarize our position in a few sentences. So, while I would prefer to start our conversation by hearing your story, I completely understand why you might want to know my views first.

I am a Christian. Among other things, that means I believe God created the world and had a design, an intention, for everything he created. I believe our world is marred by sin, so nothing operates exactly as God intended. I believe that when our bodies and souls resist God's design this is sometimes sin (like selfishness and pride) and sometimes suffering (like cancer and many forms of depression). But whenever we live outside God's design, it always creates temptation and confusion.

I also believe God gives each of us the freedom to choose what to do with him. So if I express my beliefs in a way that makes you feel I'm putting expectations on you, then I've over-stepped my bounds. I don't want to do that. I want you to see me as a safe person to talk to because I'd genuinely like to know your story.

This is an attempt to be an "openly Christian friend" who neither hides nor imposes their personal beliefs. It tries to broaden the discussion to include suffering as well as sin, and recognizes how personal beliefs should never be imposed on others. It is important to be safe before you try to be convincing. Whether or not this individual embraces the gospel is between them and God, and should not determine whether you seek to be a good friend.

Friend: That is both more and less clear than I hoped. But it seems like a fair place to start. *[Your friend shares his story. You ask well-informed questions. Good questions allow for loneliness and hurt to be shared in a non-defensive way. During this time, you don't offer much opinion but you do express empathy. Eventually your friend speaks of how his parents reacted poorly to the disclosure.]* My father asked me not to embarrass the family by telling anyone, and my mother started crying, saying I was robbing her of grandchildren! How was I not supposed to be hurt?

Before reading further, try to formulate your response at this point.

_____

_____

_____

_____

You: It hurts me to hear you tell that story. I'm sure it was incredibly painful when your parents said those things. You know, in our pain we all tend to be self-centered, and it sounds like that's exactly how your parents reacted. In that moment they were thinking more about their own lives than about yours. I'm not sure how I would respond if I were in their place either, and that unsettles me. Your father's request seems unfair and your mother's accusation implies you have a motive that obviously doesn't fit. Have things gotten better since their initial reaction?

> *This is not the time to flip the conversation by saying something like, "Your choices impact more than you, you know?" Your friend has already wrestled with the fact that his coming out has social implications and raises issues about biological children. If you try to press that home here it will feel like a cheap shot and the opposite of friendship.*

Friend: No, things haven't gotten much better. We can have surface-level conversations, but that's about it. I can tell they're trying to figure out who among their friends might have heard that I've come out. We used to argue about whether they would attend my wedding if I got married. They never said they wouldn't, but they didn't say they would either, and that was bad enough. Would you come to my wedding, or do you think my happiness is a violation of *your* ethics, too?

You: I didn't know we were already close enough for me to make the invite list ☺. We can talk about whether I might go, but my initial question would be: does attendance at a wedding mean the same thing to you that it does to your parents? It sounds like, to you, their attendance would be saying that they want you to be happy.

But for them, it would be saying that they see nothing wrong with your relationship.

Two comments here. First, whether you use humor with your friend should depend on your personality and how the two of you relate. Second, remember the levels of conversation from chapter five? When your friend asked about whether you would come to his wedding, he was asking for commitment on an action step before the two of you had agreed on facts, definitions, or values. Your follow-up question seeks to back the conversation up to the definitions level. That will allow both your conversation with him and his conversation with his parents to be more productive. In conversations like this, it is not wise to sacrifice a real friendship over a hypothetical invitation.

Friend: But why can't they just want me to be happy? Is that too much to ask?

Before reading further, try to formulate your response to this question.

_____

_____

_____

_____

You: Unless there's some big news you haven't told me, it doesn't look like you're getting married soon, so in that sense I want to be careful not to unduly harm our friendship over something that is not imminent. But I fear the question you just asked can't take our conversation in a good direction. You're concerned that your parents, by *not yet* making a decision about attending your wedding, are in a way imposing their beliefs on you. At the same time, though, you believe there's only one right decision they *could* make — they should come to your wedding as a way of saying that they want you to be happy. When you insist on that decision, you're imposing your beliefs on them, too. So if you and I keep going down the road on this all-or-nothing question, our whole conversation will end up being just a sequel to the debate you're having with your parents. I'm hoping our conversation can be more than that.

Friend: Fair enough, but I get the sense you agree with my parents. Anyway, isn't this an all-or-nothing question? Either they would attend or they wouldn't. You're not proposing one come in support and the other not attend to honor their faith, are you?

You: That would be awkward. And, no, that's not what I'm proposing, because I'm not proposing anything. It just seems to me that your family is trying to decide on actions steps prematurely. What I mean is you're not on the same page about the things that lead us to take one action or another. I doubt you and your parents agree on whether same-sex attraction was a choice for you [fact], whether marriage is a legal right or divine institution [definition], and the significance of attending a wedding [values]. These are conversations you and I haven't had, yet we're trying to decide what to do with a wedding invitation that hasn't been written. At this stage in our friendship, if you'll let me call it that, debating positions actually isn't helpful. I'd much rather know more of your story than have an all-or-nothing debate. I want us to be more like friends having a conversation than we are representatives of opposing positions.

> *You may not be this conversationally comfortable with the distinctions between facts, definitions, values, and action steps. Nevertheless, I hope this helps you see the value of these categories for those times when a conversation threatens to become a debate. Later we'll address the wedding-attendance question, but this interaction is meant to be an example of how to navigate a hypothetical topic that could derail a friendship.*

Friend: I don't think a relationship with my parents should be that complicated, but I see your point about our conversation. What do you want to know about my story?

You: Your experience of same-sex attraction seems to be a big part of your story. If you don't mind, tell me about that. When did you first begin to experience this, and what has it been like to grow up feeling like a sexual minority,[21] if it's okay for me to put it that way? Please, if I say anything offensive, I hope you'll trust me enough to tell me so I can better understand. I've not had a lot of these conversations so I may be clumsy at times.

Friend: If I'm right about what you really believe, I'm probably more okay with the term "sexual minority" than you are, but yes, I will tell you if something offends me instead of assuming you meant to be offensive. [*You friend talks about the experience of discovering his own SSA and growing up with that burden. He shares some of the key markers discussed in chapter four. You ask some informed questions, demonstrating a desire to be aware, and trust builds.*] Now, can I ask you a question, and you give me a straight answer? You keep saying "same-sex attraction" when I'm saying "gay." What's the deal?

You: I think that's a great question. The little bit I've read about homosexuality says there is benefit to distinguishing between experience, identity, and behavior. "Same-sex attraction" is an *experience*. "Gay" is a matter of *identity*, and in many cases that identity implies various forms of physical affection, which are obviously *behaviors*. What I struggle to understand, however, is a particular cultural phenomenon we're seeing. One the one hand, society usually calls it prejudice when we define or categorize or label people mainly by a single attribute — maybe that attribute is Asian or female or Southerner or Muslim. But if that attribute is same-sex attraction, things are different. If the person doesn't put his or her gay label front and center, then they may be accused of being inauthentic. And if other people don't embrace the label, they're being offensive. I'm not bringing this up as a "gotcha question." Honestly I'm confused why it happens, so I'd appreciate your thoughts.

> *This is an attempt to show how you can raise important points in a way that doesn't look like you're going for a "slam dunk." Your goal should be to present your positions with a confidence that's essentially humble rather than essentially proud.*

Friend: I thought that was where you were headed with your language. On that cultural observation, it's hard not to hear it as a "gotcha question" because it's hard to view my sexuality as just an experience. When it feels like I have to defend myself to anyone who thinks it's sinful to be gay—and when I've felt like I've had to keep my "attractions," as you call them, secret for so long—it seems like much more than an experience. When your sense of attraction has been illegal, it feels like a cause.

You: That's really helpful for me to hear. It helps me relate to what you've faced. I can definitely see where it seems lightweight to you to consider SSA as just an experience. But how do you feel about my perception—if it's even accurate—that homosexual attractions play a much larger role in your identity than heterosexual attractions play in mine?

> *There are good points to be made on both sides of these kinds of discussions. It's important to acknowledge our friend's good points if we want them to acknowledge ours. You do not want to be seen as manipulative and disingenuous as you build a friendship.*

Friend: That's a big assumption on your part, but I can see your point. To me it feels like social pressure more than choice. When I'm honest about my life, this is what stands out. It's like if I were seven feet tall, I would get a lot of questions about basketball. I don't know how to be honest about being gay in a straight world and that not be "my thing." I also know how hard it was for me to be honest, and I don't want my silence to make it harder for the next generation to feel the same silencing shame I did.

You: I think your day-to-day choices mean a lot more to you than mine do to me. I don't live with the pressure of representing a group of people. That makes sense of much of the sensitivity I perceive in the gay and lesbian community.

Friend: I appreciate your willingness to acknowledge that. Now can I ask you to really answer my other question? Since we are becoming friends and I might actually invite you to my wedding, would you come?

Before reading further, try to formulate your response to this question.

_____

_____

_____

_____

You: I don't really know at this point, and I know that's hard for you to hear. But here's an idea. How about if I share with you how I think about that question, and you can give me some perspective on my thought process? Would you be willing to offer that?"

When a conversation comes to a point that's difficult to navigate, the friendship can easily be harmed if things aren't handled well. In those moments, it can defuse some of the tension to invite a critique of your thoughts.

Friend: You're right. It's very hard to hear. But yes, I'd like to know how you think things through. It would be less personal than hearing it from my parents.

You: For me, the question begins with, *what is marriage?* I view marriage as something God created for a purpose and with guidelines. To me it's not simply a legal status recognized by the state with certain tax benefits. That's why I understand attendance at a wedding to be an endorsement of a relationship. But, as I hope you can tell, I value our friendship so I wouldn't want my beliefs about marriage to come across as a rejection of *you*. If my actions led to the severing of our friendship, that would be very painful to me.

Friend: So, you wouldn't come either?

You: Possibly not. The more our conversations can reduce the possibility of my presence at your wedding being misinterpreted, however, the more likely I would be to attend. It's not that my beliefs are more important than your day. I know it could seem that way. It's just that I am responsible for my actions *and* their message, to the extent I'm able to clarify the message. I wouldn't want my attendance to misrepresent what I believe to be God's design for marriage. Ultimately, if I came, I'd like to know that my attendance would be seen as a statement *for* something—God's willingness to meet us where we are.

Friend: So you think gay marriage is wrong, and I would be living in sin? You would only come if everyone there who knows you was aware that you did not agree with gay marriage?

You: To the second question, yes with a clarification. My faith is the most important thing about me. I don't want to hide that any more than you want to be secret about your sense of attraction. If someone asked me a question at your wedding about whether I thought the opportunity for the wedding was a good thing, I would not lie. I would speak about our friendship, about my desire for your happiness, *and* about my beliefs. You should know all that before you invited me—and if you were to decide against it, I would absolutely not be offended. Because of that, I doubt our differing beliefs would lead us to decide it was wise for me to attend. But in that case, I would want an opportunity to bless you and your spouse after your honeymoon, possibly with a dinner, as a way to continue our friendship. I would have to trust that, at that point, the sincerity of our friendship would be greater than any hurt based on my not attending your wedding.

What is your critique of how this position was articulated and the criteria on which it was based?

_____

_____

_____

_____

Friend: So you really believe gay marriage is wrong?

You: I believe God created sex and marriage for the purpose of being one man and woman for life, and that any sex outside of marriage is wrong. I believe we live in a broken world where many things don't operate according to God's intention. This results in much brokenness and confusion, which saddens me. The more I see that brokenness or suffering in my life and the lives of my friends, the sadder suffering and brokenness makes me.

Friend: Do you believe I'm going to hell?

You: Whether any individual goes to heaven or hell is not a matter of their sexuality—and for what it's worth, there will be far more heterosexuals in hell than homosexuals. It angers me whenever I hear someone say, "There will be a special place in hell for [insert any group]." If you've heard anyone say those kinds of things about the gay community, I apologize on their behalf. It's bigoted and wrong. There will also be in heaven many who experienced same-sex attraction all their lives. Where an individual spends eternity is a matter of whether they accept what Jesus did on the cross as the substitution for the debt of their sin. All sin bears the same penalty; it requires the same payment. But that gets us well ahead of ourselves. I don't expect anyone to appreciate what God did to rescue us before they have an appreciation for God creating everything with a purpose and the implications of that purpose being violated. Without that foundation, God does seem arbitrarily mean. I'm not asking you to believe what I believe now, but as much as you're interested, I would like to continue having these conversations.

> *This is another attempt to demonstrate how the facts-definitions-values-actions material from chapter five can help prevent conversations from coming to an ultimatum point—a fork in the road where it seems like the whole friendship hinges on the next answer. While God's view on marriage is unchanging, friendship for Christians should be patient.*

Friend: You want to tell me I'm going to hell and still be my friend?

You: I don't believe your sexuality is the most important thing about you any more than my sexuality is the most important thing about me. Yes, I want to have many friends who see life differently from me. I want to learn from them—you've already taught me a great deal—and I want to influence them, too. But if we mostly just debate sexuality, I don't think that would be much of a friendship. I would also want to have fun together and be able to encourage you when seasons of life are hard, because we all get those seasons.

This interaction is too brief for its intent. It is meant to reinforce the idea that friendship must be bigger than one subject—or it's not a friendship. It is easy for the subject of homosexuality to dominate a relationship, so you should regularly invite your friend to do or talk about things that don't involve sexual orientation.

Friend: Yeah, I'm not sure. Can I ask you another question about your beliefs? You seem offensive and safe at the same time, if you don't mind me offending you, too. How do you understand those passages in the Bible that condemn homosexuals?

Before reading further, try to formulate your response to this question.

_____

_____

_____

_____

You: I'm happy to continue our conversations, and it's great that you're willing to ask me a question like that. To start, I don't approve of everything Christians have done in the name of the Bible. I'm sure you know more than I do about the history of Christians going too far in that area, and I would like to learn more about that. I can also imagine that Christians have often been obnoxious about what we believe. Again, I apologize on behalf of my fellow Christians for anything like that you have experienced. But I think I may understand how you feel about the passages you're talking about. There are passages in the Bible that condemn the sins I struggle with, too, and I have this grateful dislike for them. I like my sin, or I wouldn't do it—but I don't *want* to like my sin. I wish I were not prone to it. I agree with God that I'd be better off if I didn't do, believe, or feel those things, but the natural tendencies of my heart push me toward them. I feel bad about my sin and I often wish God would leave me alone, but at the same time I'm incredibly glad he doesn't. I can imagine these experiences would all be more pronounced if I experienced SSA. However, if you wanted to study the Bible together, I think it would be more profitable at first to study passages on the gospel, the big picture of what the Bible is about, rather than passages on homosexuality, but I'd be open to either.

Friend: I'm not sure I'm up for a Bible study yet. But, are you saying your sin is just like my sin?

Before reading further, try to formulate your response to this question.

_____

_____

_____

_____

You: Yes and no. First, I view unwanted SSA as suffering, not sin. It is the context in which people are tempted to adopt a gay identity or engage in homosexual behaviors, which I do think the Bible calls sin. But I don't believe homosexuality makes it harder for someone to gain God's approval—in that sense you might say that

God doesn't have a sexual preference. What I mean is that no sin needs more of God's forgiveness than another, and God never hesitates to forgive when we repent. But I also recognize that every expression of sin is unique. Anger shows up when we don't get what we want and never thinks it's wrong. Addiction puts down roots in our body chemistry, making it much harder to break free. Insecurity tempts us to hide our real selves, cutting us off from the cure of being truly loved. Even in my brief conversation with you, I've been learning more about what makes homosexuality unique. It seems like our experiences are very similar in some ways and very different in others. That is part of what I enjoy about our friendship. Learning from you helps me get to know myself better.

Friend: So you would want me to study the Bible with you? Does that mean you want me to join your church? Is that even allowed?

You: You would be very welcome at my church. I would be happy to introduce you to my friends. You could decide if you wanted to entrust them with your experience of SSA. But if you did, I would be fine with it. It would be great to have you be part of my small group where we study the Bible together and encourage one another. My initial invitation was to study the Bible together just the two of us, but it can be as broad as you like. As for church membership, that would have to do with things like whether you agreed with the teachings of our church, which include the differences between SSA, gay identity, and homosexual behaviors. The experience of SSA would not preclude you from being a member. But, if you are interested in coming, those are all bridges I'd be happy to cross with you when the time comes. For now, know you'd be very welcome.

Two points are emphasized in this interaction. First, you're allowing your friend to decide what he shares and when. Second, you're assuring him that you are still willing to be his friend if he opens up at church about his SSA. This approach is meant to make the invitation to explore Christianity safe.

Friend: Your church wouldn't expect me to change my orientation? Would they say I have to be single for the rest of my life?

You: Wow, that's a really vulnerable question. About the expectation to change your orientation, nobody at the church has lost their "sin orientation," if it's okay for me to say it that way. Honestly, I'm not sure how much flexibility there is in someone's sexual orientation. I'm sure you've studied that more than I have. What our church expects of members is to agree with God about what is sin and remain committed to repenting of sin when we succumb to it. As for remaining single, I would think there are many factors in that decision. But let me be clear that you could absolutely be open with your experience of SSA and be a member of our church. We're not a "don't ask, don't tell" church. Now, in keeping with our understanding of Scripture, our church would remove someone from membership if they had ongoing sex outside of a biblical marriage, regardless of whether that was a same-sex romantic relationship, pre-marital sex, or a heterosexual affair. But we would want to be a family for you. In fact, "family" is one of the primary images God uses to help communicate what he wants a church to be. If you want to see if we actually live up to that, you're welcome to attend for as long as you like.

Friend: Thanks, but I think this is enough for me for

now. I appreciate the conversation, but I think I've got plenty to think about for now.

You: Me too. I've learned a lot in our conversation and will be thinking about it a great deal, I'm sure. Know that the invitations to study the Bible together or to be a guest at our church are always open. But for now, would you like to catch a movie this weekend, just to have some lighter fun together?

* * *

Conclusion

I hope this condensed dialogue didn't seem too hokey or contrived. Again, given the constraints of a brief book, the pace is artificially accelerated and there are too many topics per paragraph. Real conversations will be different.

The dialogue also doesn't wrap up nicely. In real life, friendship entails a series of conversations with no known outcome. If you feel compelled to tie up all the loose ends in every conversation, you'll present Christianity in a way that is triumphalistic. Progressive sanctification—the doctrine that we become like Christ over time instead of all at once—means that every question leads to another. We must be willing to engage these and all other conversations with the patience this doctrine requires.

As you reach the conclusion of this book, here is what I hope you've gained:

1. A genuine desire to have friends who experience SSA
2. An appreciation for the experience of SSA (recognizing that every person's story is unique) which allows you to ask good questions

3. A growing comfort level with how to express your Christian faith in conversations with friends who experience SSA

I pray that those in the church who experience SSA will feel increasingly safe to share their experience and allow their church to care for them. I also pray that unchurched individuals who experience SSA will be increasingly surprised at the quality of friendship they can have with their Christian classmates, colleagues, and family members.

Thank you for being a part of the answer to these prayers. Please continue caring. This will serve your friends well (those who experience SSA and those who are opposite-sex attracted), it will help you grow in your faith, and it will strengthen your local church through the presence and gifts of individuals who experience SSA.

Endnotes

1. This book's primary audience is the evangelical church member who experiences opposite-sex attraction (OSA) and wants to become a better friend for family members, classmates, and colleagues who experience SSA. The "we" language of this book reflects this audience and is not intended to create any "us-them" alienation among readers who experience SSA. I apologize for any emotional barriers this language may create and hope this clarification can mitigate their effects.

2. In this reference I am not condoning the "sizing of sin," but recognizing the weight of the cultural debate that exists. It is clear that Jesus did not "size sin" or he would not have lived as he did, so neither should we. But he was willing to walk across the most stark cultural divides of his day to be a vessel of the gospel—and so should we.

3. Later we will address how to build a friendship with someone who is confident they want to embrace a gay identity. I believe it is most helpful if we begin with the assumption of sexual confusion. This is where most people who experience same-sex attraction begin their journey and is, therefore, the first opportunity of the church to represent Christ well.

4. You may wonder if this view is an expression of the Pelagian heresy. I do not believe it is, but I can understand the concern. There are many dispositional struggles resulting from the fall, such as dyslexia or Asperger's, which Christians agree are suffering rather than sin. This not to equate SSA with a disability. Rather, it is to illustrate that unchosen dispositional struggles which hamper living according to God's design for human flourishing can become a source of many temptations, yet these are commonly recognized as not being sinful in themselves. As you read, I hope you come to appreciate that not all our personal experiences resulting from the fall need to be classified as sin, and some of the ways God cares for us in these experiences of suffering.

5. Grayson's story is fictional, not that of a particular individual. I acknowledge that no case study will capture "the gay experience" because there is no such thing as a monolithic gay experience any more than there is a monolithic male experience, black experience, or farmer experience. Turning a story into a stereotype is unhelpful and offensive. Please be

careful not to read this story as such.

6. October 11 is the anniversary of the 1987 National March on Washington for Lesbian and Gay Rights.

7. In this case, it was more British cultural conservatives than British Christians who were involved in this tragedy, but the Christian voice would have been a subset of the population who enacted and upheld these laws.

8. If you are studying this book in a small-group setting, be mindful of how you share these examples. If someone in the room experiences SSA or has a friend who does, it should be clear to them that you are not proud of or amused by these memories.

9. Is there a place in conversation for exhortation and warning? Of course. Warning and admonition are not mutually exclusive from a loving relationship, but warning and exhortation happen best within the context of an abiding friendship.

10. It is not a goal of this book to discuss the specific causes of same-sex attraction. However, for more information in this area I encourage you to consult some of the resources noted in chapter two, particularly the writings of Mark Yarhouse.

11. In a book on friendship, it may seem odd at first to emphasize influence. Yet friendship and influence are actually inseparable (Proverbs 17:17). If a friend confides an area of sin or temptation, we should want our role in his or her life to be redemptive. In fact, if that's not part of our goal, we're falling short of what God asks of a friend. At the same time, if the desire to influence becomes heavy-handed or takes the lead in the relationship, then we are trying to leverage the relationship rather than trusting God to use the friendship. This dishonors our friend and misrepresents God.

12. Rosaria Champagne Butterfield, *The Secret Thoughts of an Unlikely Convert* (Pittsburgh, PA: Crown & Covenant Publishers, 2012), 31.

13. Ibid., 10.

14. These markers are identified by Mark Yarhouse in his book, *Understanding Sexual Identity* (Grand Rapids: Zondervan, 2013), but I may develop these concepts differently than Dr. Yarhouse.

15. Just as someone's fear that he or she has committed the unpardonable sin is evidence that their conscience is not so seared to make this a realistic concern.

16. Equating homosexuality with hyper-emotionality is offensive

and not what is being communicated in this illustration.

17. How much change in one's sexual attraction is possible will vary significantly from person to person.This is not a book about changing one's sexual attractions but building friendships that contribute to our mutual pursuit of God's design in every area of our lives. For resources related to the efficacy of various counseling approaches related to SSA I would point you to *www.sexualidentityinstitute.org*.

18. Even when clichés and platitudes do speak a kind of generalized truth, we usually don't see them as applying to us personally.

19. Where "unnatural" refers to things not in keeping with God's design for human flourishing.

20. These would be a) that God is the Creator of all things and, therefore, defines how we should live, b) that people are both born in sin—have a fallen nature—and commit personal sins which separate us from God, c) that Jesus was God in the flesh and lived the perfect life we should live and died the death our sin deserved, d) faith in the death and resurrection of Jesus Christ as the only means to remedy our sinful condition and restore us to a right relationship with God.

21. The term "sexual minority" here is used to denote personal experience rather than political implications. SSA is a minority experience, meaning it is not the majority human experience, and this has emotional, sociological, and developmental implications that need some language in order to be recognized.

The Company We Keep
In Search of Biblical Friendship

by Jonathan Holmes
Foreword by Ed Welch

Biblical friendship is deep, honest, pure, tranparent, and liberating.

It is also attainable.

112 pages
bit.ly/B-Friend

"Jonathan Holmes has the enviable ability to say a great deal in a few words. Here is a wonderful primer on the nature of biblical friendship—what it means and why it matters."
Alistair Begg, Truth for Life; Senior Pastor, Parkside Church

"Jonathan has succeeded in giving us a picture of how normal, daily, biblical friend-ships can be used by God to mold us into the likeness of Christ. If you want a solid, fresh way of re-thinking all of your relationships, read this book."
Dr. Tim S. Lane, co-author, How People Change

"A robust and relevant GPS for intentional and vulnerable gospel-centered friendships...a great book not only for individuals, but also for small groups...a signifi-cant contribution to the Kingdom."
Robert W. Kellemen, Exec. Dir., Biblical Counseling Coalition

"Short. Thoughtful. Biblical. Practical. I'm planning to get my friends to read this book so we can transform our friendships."
Deepak Reju, Pastor of Biblical Counseling, Capitol Hill Baptist

"Filled with answers that are equally down-to-earth, nitty-gritty, and specific...taking us where we need to go with warmth and wisdom."
Wesley Hill, author, Washed and Waiting

Who Am I?
Identity in Christ

by Jerry Bridges

Jerry Bridges unpacks Scripture to give the Christian eight clear, simple, interlocking answers to one of the most essential questions of life.

91 pages
bit.ly/WHOAMI

"Jerry Bridges' gift for simple but deep spiritual communication is fully displayed in this warm-hearted, biblical spelling out of the Christian's true identity in Christ."

J. I. Packer, Theological Editor, ESV Study Bible; author, Knowing God, A Quest for Godliness, Concise Theology

"I know of no one better prepared than Jerry Bridges to write *Who Am I?* He is a man who knows who he is in Christ and he helps us to see succinctly and clearly who we are to be. Thank you for another gift to the Church of your wisdom and insight in this book."

R.C. Sproul, founder, chairman, president, Ligonier Ministries; executive editor, Tabletalk magazine; general editor, The Reformation Study Bible

"*Who Am I?* answers one of the most pressing questions of our time in clear gospel categories straight from the Bible. This little book is a great resource to ground new believers and remind all of us of what God has made us through faith in Jesus. Thank the Lord for Jerry Bridges, who continues to provide the warm, clear, and biblically balanced teaching that has made him so beloved to this generation of Christians."

Richard D. Phillips, Senior Minister, Second Presbyterian Church, Greenville, SC

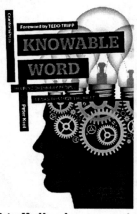

Knowable Word
Helping Ordinary People Learn to Study the Bible

by Peter Krol
Foreword by Tedd Tripp

Observe...Interpret...Apply

Simple concepts at the heart of good Bible study. Learn the basics in a few minutes—gain skills for a lifetime. The spiritual payoff is huge...ready?

108 pages   bit.ly/Knowable

"Peter Krol has done us a great service by writing the book Knowable Word. It is valuable for those who have never done in-depth Bible study and a good review for those who have. I look forward to using this book to improve my own Bible study."

Jerry Bridges, author, The Pursuit of Holiness, and many more

"It is hard to over-estimate the value of this tidy volume. It is clear and uncomplicated. No one will be off-put by this book. It will engage the novice and the serious student of Scripture. It works as a solid read for individuals or as an exciting study for a small group."

Tedd Tripp, pastor and author (from the Foreword)

"At the heart of *Knowable Word* is a glorious and crucial conviction: that understanding the Bible is not the preserve of a few, but the privilege and joy of all God's people. Peter Krol's book demystifies the process of reading God's Word and in so doing enfranchises the people of God. I warmly encourage you to read it.."

Dr. Tim Chester, The Porterbrook Network

"Here is an excellent practical guide to interpreting the Bible. Krol has thought through, tested, and illustrated in a clear, accessible way basic steps in interpreting the Bible, and made everything available in a way that will encourage ordinary people to deepen their own study."

Vern Poythress, Westminster Theological Seminary

CPSIA information can be obtained
at www.ICGtesting.com
Printed in the USA
FFOW05n0108030316